Yugoslavia's Foreign Trade

Ryan C. Amacher

The Praeger Special Studies program—utilizing the most modern and efficient book production techniques and a selective worldwide distribution network—makes available to the academic, government, and business communities significant, timely research in U.S. and international economic, social, and political development.

Yugoslavia's Foreign Trade
A Study of
State Trade Discrimination

PRAEGER SPECIAL STUDIES IN INTERNATIONAL ECONOMICS AND DEVELOPMENT

Praeger Publishers   New York   Washington   London

PRAEGER PUBLISHERS
111 Fourth Avenue, New York, N.Y. 10003, U.S.A.
5, Cromwell Place, London S.W.7, England

Published in the United States of America in 1972
by Praeger Publishers, Inc.

Library of Congress Catalog Card Number: 73-182986

Printed in the United States of America

This book examines Yugoslavia's recent experience in foreign trade in an attempt to understand more fully the reforms as they relate to international trade. Recent events clearly demonstrate the Yugoslav goal of an independent nation, integrated into world markets. If this study sheds some light on this recent experience, thereby making future developments more understandable, it will have been successful.

The study is a slightly revised version of my doctoral dissertation submitted to the James Wilson Department of Economics, University of Virginia. This origin indicates the debt of gratitude owed to many people whom I mention without implicating. The study owes much to Professor Alexander Bajt, University of Ljubljana, and Professor Ljubisa Adamovich, University of Belgrade, who both offered encouragement at a very early stage. Professors Leland Yeager and John Moore, members of my dissertation committee, gave kindly and wise guidance throughout. Many of my fellow graduate students at the University suffered through discussions on the subject matter. In particular, David Barton deserves mention for his interest and valuable comments.

I was aided in the computational work by Sandy Brown and Vicki Leonhard. Betty Tillman prepared the final manuscript. Their assistance is gratefully acknowledged. Finally, I would like to thank my wife, Susan, without whom this study would never have been completed. She edited, typed, keypunched, and, above all else, was a constant source of encouragement. For these reasons, I dedicate the study to her.

Page

LIST OF TABLES AND FIGURES

TABLES IN THE APPENDIXES

LIST OF FIGURES

Yugoslavia's Foreign Trade

1

INTRODUCTION
AND PLAN OF WORK

In recent years there has been an increase in the attention given to the foreign trade relations of socialist countries. This interest, kindled by the appearance of data heretofore unavailable, was initially a result of suspicions that the Soviet Union exploited the satellites via her powerful state trading monopoly. This view, widely held by Western economists, has been strongly denied by the Soviets.* Even within the bloc, contradictory statements may be gathered. V. Pertot of the University of Ljubljana (Yugoslavia) reports that "every new contract [in trade with Comecon] offers new possibilities for price fixing, which at a given moment, can be of a certain advantage for one of the contracting parties. . . ."[1] The Soviet view, exemplified in the words of F. Abramov, objects to any contention that monopolistic power is exerted by the state trading monopolies. He argues that " . . . the union of Eastern nations reflects a true 'brotherhood of nations' in which the major principle is 'mutual profitability.' "[2] Yugoslavia's unique position and comprehensive data allow us to examine the "discrimination hypothesis" in detail.**

---

*The literature on state trading and discrimination is reviewed in detail in Chapter 5.

**Yugoslavia's position is unique in that Yugoslavia is a "halfway house" in European trading relations. She is associated with both the CMEA (Council for Mutual Economic Assistance—Comecon) and the EEC (European Economic Community) but is a full member of neither. Yugoslavia is also unique among the socialist countries in that she makes public extremely detailed trade statistics.

A study of Yugoslavia's trade relations may reveal many interesting implications concerning the international trade of socialist
economies. The "Yugoslav experiment" is an attempt to find solutions
to problems plaguing many of the countries of Eastern Europe and the
underdeveloped world. The Yugoslav experience in international trade,
interesting in its own right, may be indicative of a trend that will be
followed by other "reform movements" as they relate to international
trade.

The purpose of this study is thus twofold: to trace the development
of Yugoslavia's foreign trade sector, and to examine the effects of
state trading on Yugoslavia's terms of trade vis-à-vis the Comecon
nations. The questions we will be seeking to answer may be put as
follows:

1. International Trade and Economic Reform

   a. How important is foreign trade to Yugoslavia (relative
to other countries)?

   b. What is Yugoslavia's relative position in "Eastern" and
"Western" trade?

   c. What is the commodity composition of Yugoslav trade?

   d. Has this commodity composition changed over time
(if so, how)?

   e. What is the direction of Yugoslav trade?

   f. Has this direction changed (if so, how)?

   g. In what ways was the Economic Reform applied to the
foreign trade sector?

   h. Have economic reforms caused any changes in the
pattern of Yugoslav trade?

2. State Trading and Discrimination

   a. How do Yugoslavia's terms of trade with Eastern Europe
compare to her terms of trade with Western Europe?

   b. Have the terms of trade changed over time?

c. How much of the observed differentials (if they exist) can be labeled "discrimination"?

d. Is there any economic explanation for the observed discrimination in intrabloc trade?

PLAN OF WORK

In attempting to answer these questions, the following plan is used. The book is divided into two parts. The first is primarily a descriptive study of Yugoslavia's international trading relations. The second is an examination of the "profitability" of Yugoslavia's trade with the bloc countries vis-à-vis her trade with Western Europe.

Part I consists of three chapters. Chapter 2 is presented as background to the present trading relations of Yugoslavia. It briefly highlights the effect that history, geography, and tradition have had on Yugoslavia's trading experience. Chapter 3 traces the development of Yugoslavia's trade sector. In this chapter we examine, in detail, changes in the composition and direction of Yugoslavia's exports and imports. Effects of the recent reform movement on international trade are discussed in Chapter 4. It is here that we "sense" a distinct difference in Yugoslavia's trading relations with East and West.

Part II examines the effects of these differences in trade with the two blocs. Chapter 5 reviews the literature of state trading and relates it to the Yugoslav experience. In Chapter 6 a model used to analyze the Yugoslav data is developed and the results are presented. In Chapter 7 several objections raised in previous studies are discussed. A simple model of trade dependence is tested.

In Chapter 8 an attempt is made to place the Yugoslav experience in perspective by summarizing the book and reviewing its conclusions. Several Appendixes containing statistical data and supplementary evidence are attached.

NOTES

1. V. Pertot, "Yugoslavia's Economic Relations with Eastern European Countries," Co-existence, IV (January 1967), 11.

2. Franklyn D. Holzman, "More on Soviet Bloc Trade Discrimination," Soviet Studies, XVII (July 1965), 64.

INTERNATIONAL TRADE
AND ECONOMIC REFORM

2

The purpose of this chapter is to provide background material for the study. To accomplish such a Herculean task in a few pages is perhaps impossible, but to say nothing would be to ignore the effect that history, geography, and tradition have had on the development of Yugoslavia's economic reforms and international trade.[1] In presenting this capsule survey, brief sketches of Yugoslavia's history, territory, resources, and population will be developed. Yugoslavia's comparative position in Eastern and Western Europe will be determined. In conclusion, the early international trade of Yugoslavia will be discussed.

HISTORICAL SURVEY

Yugoslavia came into existence in 1918 as a result of the end of the Austro-Hungarian monarchy. After the country was first formed, the Serbs seized power and imposed rigid centralism. The King of Serbia became King of Yugoslavia and imposed his will with the force of the Yugoslav (Serbian) Army. There was constant political struggle, retarding the economic development of the country. Just prior to the outbreak of World War II, political reform was attempted. The royal government achieved an agreement with the Croatian Peasant Party and autonomy was given to the Croats.[2] The outbreak of World War II abruptly ended these political reforms.

When attacked by the Axis powers, Yugoslavia fell in less than two weeks. During the German occupation, communist partisans fought a resistance in the mountainous regions of Yugoslavia. The conquered area was divided by the occupying armies of Italy and Germany. A civil war broke out during this occupation.

Nine existing ideologies, openly or secretly supported by
various factions, clashed in bloody civil war. There were
Blue and White Guard in Slovenia; Ustashis, Domobrani,
and Chetniks in Croatia; Srpska Drzavna Straza and two
groups of Chetniks in Serbia; Balisti in Kosovo; VMRO in
Macedonia; and Communists all over the place. As one
could have expected, the Communists proved most skillful.
They proclaimed a "war of national liberation" and prom-
ised free elections after the victory.
        When Tito secured material and moral support from
the Western Allies, in addition to the Soviet Union, the fate
of Yugoslavia was sealed. [3]

After gaining control, the Yugoslav Communist Party quickly
set up a Stalinist prototype political and economic system. Political
opposition was silenced, and no other parties were allowed to organize.
The entire economy was centrally managed and planned.* In these
first years the Yugoslavs were under the direct influence of the Soviet
Union so much so that Stalin was able to boast: "I have only to raise
my little finger, and there will be no more Tito."[4] Tito and his party
soon learned "that nobody inherits a brave new world and that all
economic troubles besetting Yugoslavia between the wars were still
present."[5] A political movement toward the Yugoslav "own course
to socialism" was beginning to emerge.

        Certain reforms proposed at the Second Plenum of the
        Central Committee of the Yugoslav Communist Party in
        January, 1949, clearly pointed in a new direction. In his
        speech, Boris Kidric, who was to become one of the chief
        architects of the transformation of the Yugoslav economic
        system, first ridiculed the "fetishism" of administrative
        planning and then went on to argue that it should be possible,
        at least in the consumer goods sector, "to make supply and
        demand serve as instruments for planned distribution."
        The resolutions of the Plenum noted that the chief obstacle
        to improving the quality and choice of goods in socialist
        trade was the persistent reliance on administrative ration-
        ing. . . . The economic appendages of the state had
        already begun to wither away. [6]

---

*The exception was agriculture, where the large numbers of
peasants who supported the communists were opposed to collectivization, making rapid collectivization infeasible.

This led to Yugoslavia's expulsion from Cominform (The Communist Information Bureau) and the economic blockade by members of the Warsaw Pact. The expulsion was announced on June 28, 1948. The Yugoslav leaders had demonstrated "petty-bourgeois nationalism" and "boundless ambition, arrogance, and conceit." Four explicit charges were made: The Yugoslav Communist leaders had followed an un-Marxist line on major questions of home and foreign policy. They had shown an unfriendly attitude to the Soviet Union and its Communist Party. They had treated the Yugoslav peasants as one class, not discriminating against rich peasants, and had not collectivized the land. Finally, they had subordinated the Yugoslav Communist Party to the People's Front and kept the activities of that Communist Party secret as if it were still an underground organization. [7] But Tito proved to be more firmly entrenched than Stalin had thought, and Tito and Yugoslavia weathered the blockade and proceeded on their "own road to socialism."

The reform movements have waxed and waned since Yugoslavia's initial break with "conservative communism."* Bombelles points out that the early reforms "introduced several methodological innovations in the socialist economic system," but "top political leadership still made basic economic decisions. . . . The same people, having the same objectives and using basically the same strategies, continued to develop Yugoslavia." [8] Recent reforms have been more basic, granting more autonomy to the Yugoslav enterprise. As they proceed, these reforms change the basic structure of the Yugoslav brand of communism. As S. Pejovich has pointed out,

. . . the Yugoslav economic system is unique. It contains characteristics of both a centrally planned and a free market economy, and its emergence, therefore, represents a major innovation in the economics of socialism. [9]

TERRITORY AND RESOURCES

Present-day Yugoslavia comprises somewhat less than 100,000 square miles of land in Southeastern Europe. Yugoslavia, the largest Balkan state, lies on the northwestern Balkan peninsula. The land

---

*Chapter 4 will deal with the reform movements as they relate to international trade.

is cut by mountain ranges, making the terrain harsh.* These mountain ranges shut the interior of the country from the natural harbors of the coast, causing the inhabitants of Croatia and Serbia historically "to look to East and Central Europe rather than to the sea for their contacts with the outside world."10

The most economically developed areas in the country lie in the North and Northeast. These areas comprise the southern part of the Panonian lowlands crossed by the Danube, Sava, Drava, and the Tisa rivers. This is the extensively farmed, agriculturally developed area of Yugoslavia. The possibility of expanding this agricultural land is very small. In fact, due to powerful erosive forces, effort must be extended to maintain it.11

Yugoslavia is rich in hydraulic power potential and poor in coal deposits. The hydraulic potential has yet to be fully developed. Coal is present but it is almost 90 percent lignite. There are also very small quantities of petroleum. Copper, aluminum, zinc, and lead are available in such large quantities that Yugoslavia is considered one of the wealthiest countries of Europe in this area. In addition to these resources, timber is found in large quantities and the general geography and climate make the country attractive for tourism.

POPULATION

The Socialist Federal Republic of Yugoslavia** is composed of six republics. These republics are formed along ethnic lines, but these lines are not well drawn. "The Yugoslav concept of nationality is more personal than territorial in nature."12 The numerous national groups, attempting to preserve their ethnic identity, have contributed to an unstable situation.

----

*It is these mountain ranges that harbored the Yugoslav partisan forces during the German occupation and contributed to the partisan success. This success may, in part, be responsible for Yugoslavia's "own road to socialism." The early Yugoslav Communist Party was a popular front party and, as such, felt itself to be independent of the Soviet Union.

**This translates to the Socialist Federal Republic of South Slavs ("Jug" means "South").

An example of the problem caused by these numerous nationalities is the language question. Yugoslavs speak over sixteen different languages, even if Serbo-Croatian is counted as one. [13]

> Though most Slavic peoples in Yugoslavia can understand each other, they cannot all read each other's language owing to two alphabets. . . . We also note that the minority languages are totally unrelated to the Slavic languages as well as to each other. [14]

Among the population classified by mother tongues, we find Serbo-Croatian, Slovenian, Macedonian, Shqiptar (Albanian), Hungarian, Turkish, Slovak, Gypsy, Bulgarian, German, Rumanian, Ruthenian, Wallachian, Italian, Czech, and Russian.

The problems caused by these numerous nationalities and languages, when coupled with divergent levels of development between these areas, cause suspicion and rivalries that are difficult to reconcile. In fact, one of the primary goals of the government's Economic Reform has been to equalize income differentials among the republics.

LEVEL OF DEVELOPMENT

The Yugoslav economy has undergone rapid growth in the postwar period. Pre-World War II Yugoslavia had an income (measured in constant 1960 prices) of about $130 per capita and a yearly growth rate in per capita income of about 1.5 percent. [15] The economy consisted primarily of a subsistence agriculture sector. In 1938, 74.8 percent of the people were employed in agriculture with more than two-thirds of these holdings less than five hectares (a hectare equals 2.47 acres); 46.5 percent of national income came from this sector. [16] This ranked Yugoslavia among the world's most underdeveloped countries. This low level of income compares to a per capita income of $450 in 1967. [17] In recent years Yugoslavia has enjoyed one of the fastest growth rates in Eastern or Western Europe. Even with this recent rapid growth, Yugoslavia must still be listed with the less developed countries. However, this growth characterizes the Yugoslav economy as one in a "developing" or "semi-developed" situation.

Comparatively, Yugoslavia ranks as one of the least developed European countries. Table 1 lists per capita gross domestic product

(GDP) for selected countries in 1960 and 1965.* Yugoslavia ranks
only above Albania when compared to the Comecon countries.[18]
Comparing Yugoslavia to her West European trading partners presents
an even bleaker picture. Yugoslavia ranks the lowest among the West
European countries and the range of these incomes is much greater
than in East Europe. (Some areas of Yugoslavia, namely Slovenia and
Croatia, are much more developed than the rest of the country. These
areas enjoy a level of income almost twice the mean.)[19] When Yugoslavia is compared to other underdeveloped countries, the result of
her recent, rapid growth rate is visible.

FOREIGN TRADE

The pre-World War II international trade characteristics of
Yugoslavia are similar to those generally found in a less-developed
country. More than 75 percent of her exports consisted of food and
other crude materials. Over half of all her exports were of goods
that had not undergone any manufacture ("transformation"). Yugoslavia was exporting food and raw materials and importing manufactured
goods and machines. Table 2 presents measures of the trade structure
just prior to World War II. The one exception to this familiar description was the balance of trade. From 1930 until 1939, Yugoslavia
exported more than she imported. This was largely the result of the
large German demand for food and raw materials after Hitler's rise
and the subsequent German rearmament.[20]

---

*The figures in Table 1 are presented to give a comparative
"feeling" for Yugoslavia's level of income. The figures are taken
from E. Hagen and O. Hawrylyshyn (note 18); their methodology is
described in a footnote to Table 1. The authors themselves warn
against the use of their figures in anything but general comparisons:
"The Communist-non-Communist income comparison is meaningful
only for very large income differences because of the difficulty of
adapting the income data of Communist countries to Western concepts
and converting the estimate in own currencies to equivalent values
in other currencies. Because of possible errors in the procedure
used to solve these difficulties, the data in U.S. dollars for the
European Communist countries may considerably overstate the GDP
of those relative to the GDP of non-Communist countries. The
probability of understatement is very small."

TABLE 1

Income Estimates, Selected Countries, 1960 and 1965[a]

Country	1960 GDP/Capita (U.S. $)	1965 GDP/Capita (U.S. $)
Comecon		
USSR	925	1,150
Rumania	480	620
Poland	640	820
Bulgaria	510	630
Hungary	720	940
E. Germany	1,060	1,270
Czechoslovakia	1,200	1,300
Albania[b]	155	185
EEC		
Italy	677	1,100
France	1,322	1,922
W. Germany	1,338	1,977
Netherlands	979	1,532
Belgium	1,237	1,761
Luxembourg	1,594	1,915
EFTA		
Portugal	285	400
Austria	877	1,287
U.K.	1,353	1,790
Sweden	1,644	2,487
Denmark	1,299	2,109
Switzerland	1,584	2,301
Other		
Yugoslavia	235	370
Greece	410	673
Spain	337	600
Brazil	242	273
Colombia	295	305
India	78	102
Indonesia	63	70
Pakistan	77	97
Turkey	205	279
Ghana	198	288
Tunisia	189	205
Libya	131	705
U.A.R.	151	159

[a]At current market prices. "The general approach to the estimation of income, as well that of growth, was to use official data, for the most part from international agency sources. Incomes were expressed in dollars by conversion at exchange rates considered to be approximately representative of relative purchasing power in international trade, which in the majority of cases meant official exchange rates." (See Source, below, Hagen and Hawrylyshyn, p. 7.) Estimates for the communist countries were obtained in a different manner. Figures for the Soviet Union come from Stanley Cohn, "Soviet Growth Retardation," U.S., Congress, Joint Economic Committee, New Directions in the Soviet Economy: Economic Performance (Washington, D.C.: Government Printing Office, 1966), and adjusted to make them more appropriate to the other gross national income (GNI) figures. Figures for the countries of Eastern Europe (except Albania and Yugoslavia) were taken from Maurice Ernst, "Postwar Economic Growth in Eastern Europe," U.S. Congress Joint Economic Committee, New Directions in the Soviet Economy: The World Outside (Washington, D.C.: Government Printing Office, 1966). Again the figures were adjusted to account for the fact that Ernst's figures were based on the purchasing power equivalent technique. In all cases the 1965 figures were obtained by extrapolating from the 1964 figures of Cohn and Ernst. Estimates for Yugoslavia were obtained by converting Yugoslavia's own-currency GNI by official exchange rates. The estimate for Albania was made on the assumption that it was equal to that of the republic of Montenegro in Yugoslavia. As the authors state, "It should be clear from the immediately preceding statements that the dollar GDP figures for all of the Communist countries have exceptionally large margins of error." (See Source below, Hagen and Hawrylyshyn, p. 42.)
   [b]Albania was a member of Comecon from 1949 to 1962.

   Source: E. Hagen and O. Hawrylyshyn, "Analysis of World Income and Growth, 1955-1965," Economic Development and Cultural Change, Vol. XVIII, Part II (October 1969).

TABLE 2

Selected Measures of the Prewar (1939) Export-
Import Structure of Yugoslavia

Measure	Percent of Total
Exports by commodity section	
Food	43.4
Crude materials, inedible, except fuels	34.5
Exports by stage of production	
Crude materials	55.4
Exports by industry	
Nonferrous metallurgy	14.5
Wood industry	15.3
Food industry	15.1
Crop farming	12.8
Stock breeding	16.6
Forest exploitation	4.2
Imports by commodity section	
Food	5.2
Manufactured goods classified by material	40.7
Machinery and transport equipment	20.0
Imports by stage of production	
More elaborately transformed articles	53.9

Source: Statisticki Godisnjak FNRJ, 1955 (Belgrade: Federal
Statistical Administration, 1955), pp. 209-15.

     The war and its aftermath caused changes in Yugoslav foreign
transactions. Among the most noticeable was the large increase in
the import of food and food products—from 5.2 percent of all imports
in 1939 to 21.8 percent of all imports in 1952.[21] This increase was
mainly due to a large increase in the importation of cereal and cereal
products. The exports in the early postwar period still consisted of
crude articles, but there was a movement away from food export.
Nonferrous metallurgy and forest products filled the gap left by the
decline in food exports. This early post-World War II period could

be characterized as one in which the Yugoslavs lived off their forests and minerals.

The pre-World War II period and the early post-World War II period are similar in that Yugoslav exports consisted basically of raw materials and food products. The early postwar period is further affected by the experience of the Cominform blockade. It is from this characteristically underdeveloped situation that we will trace the composition, direction, and growth of Yugoslav foreign trade in Chapter 3.

NOTES

1. For more complete information concerning the social, political, and historical background of Yugoslavia see Ivan Avakumovic, History of the Communist Party of Yugoslavia (Aberdeen University Press, 1964); Joseph T. Bombelles, Economic Development of Communist Yugoslavia, 1947-1964 (Stanford: Hoover Institution Publications, 1968); Stephen Clissold, ed., A Short History of Yugoslavia (Cambridge: At the University Press, 1966); M. Heppell and F. Singleton, Yugoslavia (New York: Praeger, 1961); Frits W. Hondius, The Yugoslav Community of Nations (The Hauge: Mouton, 1968); George M. Zaninovich, The Development of Socialist Yugoslavia (Baltimore: Johns Hopkins Press, 1968).

2. Bombelles, Economic Development of Communist Yugoslavia, pp. 3, 4.

3. Ibid., pp. 7, 8.

4. Clissold, A Short History of Yugoslavia, p. 7.

5. Bombelles, Economic Development of Communist Yugoslavia, p. 11.

6. John M. Montias, "Economic Reform and Retreat in Yugoslavia," Foreign Affairs, XXXVII, 2 (1959), 295.

7. Clissold, A Short History of Yugoslavia, p. 246.

8. Bombelles, Economic Development of Communist Yugoslavia, p. 71.

9. Svetozar Pejovich, The Market-Planned Economy of Yugo-slavia (Minneapolis: University of Minnesota Press, 1966), p. ix. The effect of these dual characteristics on international trade will be the subject of Chapters 5 and 6 of this study.

10. Heppell, Yugoslavia, p. 16.

11. Milos Samardzija and Radoslav Ratkovic, "Yugoslavia: A Yugoslav Marxist View," in Harry Shaffer, ed., The Communist World: Marxist and Non-Marxist Views (New York: Appleton-Century-Crofts, 1967), p. 261.

12. Hondius, The Yugoslav Community of Nations, p. 12.

13. Ibid., p. 22.

14. Ibid., pp. 23, 24.

15. Samardzija and Ratkovic, "Yugoslavia: A Yugoslav Marxist View," p. 272.

16. Bombelles, Economic Development of Communist Yugo-slavia, p. 4.

17. Yugoslavia, OECD Economic Surveys (Geneva, Switzerland: Organization for Economic Cooperation and Development, November 1969), p. 1.

18. Everett Hagen and Oli Hawrylyshyn, "Analysis of World Income and Growth, 1955-1965," Economic Development and Cultural Change, XVIII, Part II (October 1969), pp. 3, 4.

19. Branko Colanovic, Development of the Underdeveloped Areas in Yugoslavia (Belgrade: Medunarodna Politika, 1966), p. 8.

20. Bombelles, Economic Development of Communist Yugo-slavia, p. 5.

21. Statisticki Godisnjak FNRJ, 1955 (Belgrade: Federal Institute for Statistics, 1955), p. 211.

3

THE PATTERN
OF YUGOSLAV TRADE

Chapter 3 is primarily an exercise in descriptive statistics, tracing the development of Yugoslavia's trade sector. The chapter will show how the composition and direction of Yugoslavia's trade has changed in the last decade. The first section will trace the general state of development of Yugoslavia's trading sectors; it will deal in broad aggregates and attempt to portray the trade sector of Yugoslavia, using comparative techniques. The subsequent three sections will examine Yugoslavia's economic relations with Western Europe and the United States, the Comecon countries, and the developing countries, respectively. These sections will examine the data in greater detail with particular attention to the countries involved. In concluding, we will attempt to determine if any pattern is developing in Yugoslavia's international economic relations.

YUGOSLAVIA'S TRADE POSITION

As we have seen, Yugoslavia's unique position in international economic relations has its roots in political events. In the immediate postwar period there was a general feeling in Eastern Europe that a fully planned economy should follow an autarkic policy. * Political events were to prove that Yugoslavia would not be able to pursue such an isolationist policy.

---

*The complex (and dead-end) problem of what is meant by an autarkic policy is avoided here; it makes no difference in Yugoslavia's case if country or bloc autarky, now or sometime in the future, is implied.

> In June, 1948, an adamant Stalin had a recalcitrant Yugo-
> slavia expelled from Cominform. . . . Between March
> and July, 1949, the East European Members of Comin-
> form cancelled all trade agreements with Yugoslavia and
> together with the Soviet Union began an economic blockade
> against her. Isolated from the Soviet Bloc countries, Yugo-
> slavia was now forced to seek trading with the West.[1]

Since this time, trade has been resumed between Yugoslavia and the
East European countries, but trade with the West has not ceased to
be an important part of Yugoslavia's foreign trade sector. It seems
that these external events caused the recognition that seeking development with a closed economy had to give way to specialization in a
range of commodities in which Yugoslavia could compete with the
West. This realization has stimulated trade until the present, when
political leaders are calling for still more economic integration.

Although the initial stimulus mentioned above was "forced" upon
Yugoslavia, later experience gives evidence of the deliberate effort
to cultivate international relations. Yugoslavia has actively solicited
participation in international organizations. In addition to active
membership in the United Nations, Yugoslavia is a member of the
ECE (Economic Commission for Europe) and, along with Czechoslo-
vakia and Poland, is a member of GATT (General Agreement on
Tariffs and Trade). Yugoslavia is the only Eastern European country
to be an active member of the IMF (International Monetary Fund),
IBRD (International Bank for Reconstruction and Development), and
OECD (Organization for Economic Co-Operation and Development).
Although a full member of neither, Yugoslavia is associated with
both Comecon and the EEC.[2] (An unpublished lecture by Ljubisa S.
Adamovich, University of Belgrade, serves to underscore Yugoslavia's
unique position. Adamovich argued that Yugoslavia will never be a
full member of Comecon or an associate member of the EEC; its aim
was working agreements with Comecon and preferential treatment by
the EEC. He saw Yugoslavia as a clearing place for goods between
the two blocs. Adamovich argued that the Yugoslavs recognize the
economic costs of not fully integrating into the EEC but regard them
as calculated costs of maintaining their position.)[3]

It seems this "opening" of Yugoslavia is a very deliberate policy.
The leaders of Yugoslavia have demonstrated a conscious effort to
maintain and enlarge upon its effects. This effort is exemplified in
the words of Mijalko Todorovic, Secretary of the Party Central Committee's Executive Committee. He stated

We are such a small producing community that in no case
can we provide a full assortment and quantity of goods if
we do not integrate much more decisively into the world
market.[4]

Because of this desire to integrate into the world market (or at least
the lack of a conscious effort to follow an autarkic policy), it is interesting to analyze empirically the path this integration has taken.
This section will examine the general movement of trading relations
in a comparative setting.

First, two measures of the level (importance) of Yugoslav trade
relative to similar levels in her trading partners are presented.
Table 3 presents figures for trade turnover (exports plus imports)
per capita and trade turnover as a percentage of gross domestic product (GDP) for 1965.* These measures are presented only in an attempt
to view Yugoslavia in the proper perspective. Too much attention
should not be given the particular entries with their inherent inadequacies.** The data indicate that Yugoslavia's level of trade, on a
per capita basis, is relatively low when compared to other Comecon
countries, very low when compared to the EEC and EFTA (European
Free Trade Association) countries, and moderately high when compared to a selected group of other less developed countries. The
second, more standard measure, trade turnover as a percentage of
GDP, indicates a quite different position. The level of trade relative
to the Comecon countries is quite high (only two countries are higher).
Relative to the EEC countries, the level of trade is also quite high—
higher than all countries, with the exception of Belgium-Luxembourg
and the Netherlands. In relation to the EFTA countries, Yugoslavia's
level of trade as a percentage of GDP is moderately lower than the
group as a whole.

_____

*Similar data for 1960 appears in Appendix A, Table A-1.

**These measures are weakened by all the normal inadequacies
of comparative statistics, and in particular, the different methods of
measuring GDP. These figures for trade turnover as a percent of
GDP are doubly treacherous because of the problems involved in
measuring GDP (see discussion in footnote on page 14) and official
exchange rate definitions. The reader is reminded that these figures
are presented only to develop a "sense" for the situation.

TABLE 3

Trade Turnover: Two Measures, Selected Countries, 1965

Countries	Trade Turnover, Per Capita ($ U.S.)	Trade Turnover, GDP
Comecon		
USSR	70.4	.06
Rumania	180.9	.29
Poland	145.4	.17
Bulgaria	286.7	.45
Hungary	298.6	.31
E. Germany	312.8	.24
Czechoslovakia	378.7	.29
Albania*	84.9	.45
EEC		
Italy	282.6	.25
France	416.8	.21
W. Germany	599.0	.30
Netherlands	1,127.3	.73
Belgium-Luxembourg	1,317.3	.74
EFTA		
Portugal	162.5	.40
Austria	509.8	.39
UK	528.6	.29
Norway	982.0	.51
Sweden	706.8	.43
Denmark	1,080.5	.51
Switzerland	1,118.7	.48
Other		
Yugoslavia	122.0	.32
Greece	171.2	.25
Spain	126.4	.18
Brazil	33.1	.12
Colombia	55.8	.18
India	9.5	.09
Indonesia	13.5	.19
Pakistan	15.3	.15
Turkey	31.5	.11
Ghana	95.1	.32
Tunisia	78.0	.38
Libya	690.0	1.05
UAR	51.9	.32

*Member, 1949-62.

Source: Appendix A, Table A-1.

Several insights can be drawn from this data. There seems to be a correlation between the level of development and the trade turn-over on a per capita basis. The less developed countries, almost without exception, have a lower volume of trade per capita.* It is interesting to note that among the less developed countries, Yugo-slavia's volume of trade on a per capita basis is quite high. However, it is lower than the volume of trade in the EEC and EFTA countries at any level of development. Turning to the second measure, we do not find the correlation with the level of development that existed in the first. In general it appears that the countries belonging to a customs union or free-trade area (defined very loosely) experience a higher volume of trade by this measure. In general, the data indicate that international trade plays a larger role in Yugoslavia than in most countries of its economic class. It appears that trade would probably increase in importance if Yugoslavia were to integrate more fully into either the customs union or free trade area of Western Europe.**

Having attempted to place Yugoslavia's level of trade in a com-parative setting, we will examine the course her trade relations have taken in recent years. Table 4 presents figures for the value of ex-ports and imports in the postwar period. We see that in the period 1947-69, Yugoslavia experienced a consistent deficit in her balance of trade. In 1965, the first year of the price reform, there was a marked, but short-lived, turnabout in this trend. This increasing trade deficit and the resultant deficit on current account are partly the result of the application of the 1965 reforms. The increased liberalization has boosted imports, with the export sector lagging behind. The growing surplus in the invisible balance, stimulated by the export of tourism, has worked to offset this trade deficit.***

---

*Libya appears to be a very notable exception; the USSR is also an exception among the developed countries.

**International trade is increasing at a faster rate than industrial production in both the EEC and EFTA. Changes in these two measures from 1960-65 are also presented in Appendix A, Table A-1. In the case of Yugoslavia, trade, as a percentage of GDP, did not change over the five-year period and trade turnover per capita increased 61 percent over the same period. This is in contrast to figures for the Comecon countries, which show increases in both measures for 1960-65.

***Yugoslavs were slow to develop the tourist potential of their country. This is quite probably the result of such early planning

TABLE 4

Yugoslav Exports and Imports, 1947-69
(million new dinars)*

	Imports	Exports	Balance of Trade	Export-Import Ratio (%)
1947	2,075.9	2,046.1	-29.8	98.6
1948	3,831.0	3,711.8	-119.2	96.9
1949	3,685.2	2,483.7	-1,201.5	67.4
1950	2,883.4	1,929.4	-954.0	66.9
1951	4,796.4	2,234.0	-2,562.4	46.6
1952	4,663.4	3,081.5	-1,581.9	66.1
1953	4,941.2	2,324.7	-2,616.5	47.0
1954	4,242.4	3,004.7	-1,237.7	70.8
1955	5,511.9	3,207.3	-2,304.6	58.2
1956	5,926.7	4,042.1	-1,884.6	68.2
1957	8,266.3	4,938.8	-3,327.5	59.7
1958	8,562.5	5,517.4	-3,045.1	64.4
1959	8,589.7	5,958.0	-2,631.7	69.4
1960	10,329.7	7,076.9	-3,252.8	68.5
1961	11,378.4	7,111.1	-4,267.3	62.5
1962	11,096.5	8,631.0	-2,465.5	77.8
1963	13,207.8	9,879.3	-3,328.5	74.8
1964	16,539.7	11,164.4	-5,375.5	67.5
1965	16,099.4	13,643.8	-2,455.5	84.7
1966	19,692.9	15,251.0	-4,441.9	77.4
1967	21,341.6	15,645.8	-5,695.8	73.3
1968	22,460.2	15,796.3	-6,663.9	70.3
1969	26,685.0	18,431.0	-8,254.0	69.1

*12.5 new dinars = $1.

Sources: Statisticki Godisnjak Jugoslavije, 1969 (Belgrade: Federal Institute for Statistics, 1969), p. 208; Statistika Spoljne Trgovine SFR Jugoslavije, 1969 (Belgrade: Federal Institute for Statistics, 1970), p. 17.

In concluding this very brief treatment of Yugoslavia's balance-
of-trade deficit, it is perhaps most illuminating to pay particular
attention to the export-import ratio in Table 4. This ratio has deteriorated with no exceptions from 1965, and with only one exception
since 1962.* Perhaps an encouraging note should be added. Since
1965, the rate of increase in this growing trade deficit has declined.
This fact, coupled by the increasing rate of growth in the export of
tourism, may act to dampen the balance-of-payments pressure.

We have seen how the volume of trade has increased, but with
a lagging export sector. In the remaining portion of this section, we
will examine several different measures of the growth in this volume
of trade. Trade will be examined by branch of economic activity,
use of product, degree of manufacture, and trading groups. This
disaggregation may enable us to learn what has contributed most to
this growth in the volume of trade.

Table 5 shows how the export contribution of various branches
of production has changed in recent years. Over the ten-year period,
industry has increased its share to almost 85 percent of all exports.
This increased contribution to exports has come almost exclusively
from a few sectors of the industrial branch and does not cut across
all sectors of industrial production. The branches of nonferrous
metallurgy, textiles, leather and footwear, and the chemical industry
have made the most significant contribution to the increase in the
industrial share of the export market. Shipbuilding, paper, and
rubber production have also seen increases in their relative share of
industry's increasing export participation. Several industrial branches,
however, have not maintained their relative position; indeed, some
have experienced an absolute decline in the value of their exports.
Among the most notable are the foodstuff, timber, and petroleum and
derivatives industries, which have all experienced an absolute decline

----

prejudices as the well-known fascination with heavy industry. A fear
that tourism, because of its high income elasticity, is a more volatile
export has no doubt also contributed to this slow growth.

*It is beyond the scope and intent of this section and this book
to examine the complex problems of Yugoslavia's balance of payments
problem and its interaction with recent economic reform in any greater
detail. The balance-of-payments problem seems to be responsible
for much of the reform program as it relates to international trade,
but many of these reforms have further aggravated the deficit.

TABLE 5

Branch Contribution to Exports, 1960–69

Production Branch	Percentage of Total Exports									
	1960	1961	1962	1963	1964	1965	1966	1967	1968	1969
Industry	74.8	74.7	79.0	76.6	78.3	81.2	81.5	79.2	83.3	84.4
Electric energy	0.2	0.1	0.2	0.3	0.0	0.0	0.0	0.1	0.1	0.0
Coal and coal derivatives	0.4	0.4	0.2	0.2	0.2	0.1	0.2	0.1	0.1	0.3
Crude petroleum and derivatives	0.6	1.0	2.2	1.5	1.2	0.9	1.7	1.6	0.9	0.8
Iron and steel metallurgy	3.7	3.6	4.0	2.7	2.4	1.9	1.9	2.5	2.3	2.4
Nonferrous metallurgy	10.0	9.1	9.1	8.5	9.3	9.4	9.7	8.7	11.8	13.8
Nonmetals	2.6	2.5	2.8	2.5	3.1	3.0	2.6	2.4	2.6	2.6
Metal industry	12.0	11.9	13.2	11.2	11.9	15.0	15.4	13.3	12.3	11.2
Shipbuilding	3.3	4.9	9.5	7.0	4.6	7.2	7.2	4.7	6.5	6.8
Electrical industry	4.3	4.6	4.2	4.7	4.3	5.7	6.3	6.4	6.7	6.6
Chemical industry	2.9	2.6	2.4	2.7	3.7	5.0	5.2	5.5	5.6	5.8
Building material industry	0.2	0.2	0.2	0.2	0.2	0.2	0.2	0.3	0.2	0.2
Timber industry	12.1	11.5	11.1	11.0	10.6	8.8	8.3	7.8	8.6	8.5
Paper industry	1.4	1.1	1.3	1.7	1.6	1.7	1.9	2.0	2.7	2.4
Textile industry	5.9	6.4	6.0	7.7	8.9	8.4	8.7	9.8	10.4	10.9
Leather and footwear industry	2.4	2.4	2.5	3.6	4.5	3.9	4.0	5.5	5.6	5.1
Rubber industry	0.0	0.1	0.1	0.1	0.3	0.3	0.4	0.3	0.3	0.4
Foodstuffs industry	9.2	9.4	7.0	7.2	7.2	6.3	5.1	5.7	4.5	5.0
Printing industry	0.0	0.1	0.0	0.1	0.1	0.2	0.1	0.1	0.2	0.2
Tobacco industry	3.5	2.7	3.0	3.7	4.2	3.2	2.7	2.4	2.0	1.4
Film industry	0.1	0.1	0.0	0.0	0.0	0.0	0.0	0.0	0.0	0.0
Agriculture	23.2	22.9	19.0	21.1	19.6	17.3	17.4	19.8	15.5	14.4
Agriculture	8.9	6.2	2.5	3.3	2.6	2.6	4.0	5.8	3.8	2.8
Fruits	0.5	0.6	1.2	0.7	0.9	0.4	0.3	0.4	0.2	0.5
Livestock	10.7	13.4	12.2	14.0	13.5	12.1	11.3	11.8	9.8	9.4
Fisheries	0.3	0.3	0.3	0.2	0.2	0.1	0.1	0.1	0.1	0.1
Home-produced agricultural products	2.8	2.4	2.8	2.9	2.4	2.1	1.7	1.7	1.6	1.6
Forestry	2.0	2.4	2.0	2.3	2.1	1.5	1.1	1.0	1.2	1.2
Forest exploitation	1.3	1.6	1.0	1.4	1.3	0.9	0.5	0.5	0.6	0.7
Hunting and medicinal herbs	0.7	0.8	1.0	0.9	0.8	0.6	0.6	0.5	0.6	0.5
Total	100.0	100.0	100.0	100.0	100.0	100.0	100.0	100.0	100.0	100.0

Source: Appendix A, Table A-2. For figures on movements in quantity and value following this same classification scheme, see Table A-2.

in exports (see Table A-2). The iron and steel industry has also rea-
lized a decline, but only in its relative importance as a contributor to
the export sector. This increasing importance of industrial exports
has, of course, meant that agriculture and forestry have experienced
a relative decline in their contribution to the export sector. Forestry's
share of the export market has fallen by almost 50 percent, from 2.0
percent in 1960 to 1.2 percent in 1969. The decline in agriculture has
not been as drastic but is none the less quite significant. All sectors
of the agriculture branch have seen a decline in their relative importance. The agricultural* and livestock sectors, the largest contributors
to agriculture's exports, have both experienced a large decrease in
their relative participation in the export sector.

It is clear that the Yugoslav export bundle has changed and that
this change is in the direction of greater reliance on the export of
industrial products. This trend would seem to indicate that the Yugoslav export sector is moving toward a mix of products more consistent
with the export sector of a developed economy. (There are various
"criteria for underdevelopedness." For example, Leibenstein's
criteria as they relate to the export sector are export of foodstuffs
and raw materials, and a low volume of trade per capita.5 Other
standard textbooks for development suggest similar criteria.)

In subjecting imports to this same type of analysis in Table 6,
we discover that one of our three classifications (reproduction goods)
has experienced a slight growth in relative importance at the expense
of the other two (investment goods, consumer goods). Closer examination of the first classification indicates that the growth has come
in the two areas of crude materials and semiproducts and manufactured
goods for reproduction; the third, mineral fuels, has only maintained
its relative share of the import bundle. Goods for reproduction now
account for three-fifths of all Yugoslav imports. This figure, particularly the contribution of crude materials and semiproducts, is
likely to rise as Yugoslavia continues to industrialize.

Turning to the two categories that are decreasing in their relative
share of imports, we find that in the first, investment goods and equipment, there has been a marked decline in the importation of transport

---

*The statistical yearbook does not go into detail concerning the
composition of the agriculture sector of the agriculture branch. However, by elimination it must consist of grain-and-dairy-product production.

TABLE 6

Use of Imports, 1960-69

Use of Product	Use as a Percentage of Total Imports									
	1960	1961	1962	1963	1964	1965	1966	1967	1968	1969
Reproduction goods	56.8	52.3	54.3	57.7	62.5	62.1	57.5	57.2	56.9	60.2
Crude materials and semiproducts	35.5	33.4	35.4	38.7	41.7	42.0	38.0	36.7	35.6	38.7
Mineral fuels	5.5	4.4	5.4	4.5	5.0	5.6	5.2	5.0	5.5	4.8
Manufactured goods for reproduction	15.8	14.5	13.5	14.5	15.8	14.5	14.3	15.5	15.8	16.7
Investment goods and equipment	28.5	28.2	25.2	20.0	21.6	19.7	21.8	21.7	24.9	22.3
Power-generating machinery	2.8	2.2	1.5	0.7	0.7	0.5	1.2	.3	1.1	0.7
Agricultural machinery	2.9	0.3	0.3	0.4	0.7	0.6	1.0	1.3	1.1	0.9
Metal-working machinery	1.5	1.8	4.1	2.7	4.2	3.1	2.7	2.0	1.4	1.4
Other machinery	11.9	13.1	12.8	10.1	9.3	8.6	8.0	9.2	11.4	10.3
Electrical motors and other equipment	2.8	2.8	2.6	2.9	2.2	2.0	2.2	2.1	2.5	2.7
Transport equipment	5.0	6.5	2.6	1.9	2.6	3.5	4.8	4.4	4.5	3.6
Other investment	1.4	1.5	1.3	1.3	1.9	1.4	1.9	2.4	2.9	2.7
Consumer goods	14.5	19.5	20.5	22.3	15.9	18.2	20.7	21.1	18.2	17.7
Food	8.1	12.6	14.0	16.1	9.8	12.1	12.8	8.9	4.7	4.5
Beverages and tobacco	0.0	0.1	0.4	0.7	0.2	0.0	0.4	0.4	0.2	0.3
Clothing and footwear	0.4	0.5	0.5	0.4	0.4	0.4	0.4	0.9	1.4	1.3
Furniture	0.0	0.0	0.0	0.0	0.0	0.0	0.0	0.0	0.0	0.1
Textile articles (excluding footwear)	1.8	2.2	2.1	1.5	1.9	2.1	2.8	2.8	3.2	2.8
Medicinal, pharmaceutical, and cosmetic products	1.0	1.0	1.0	0.9	0.8	0.8	0.8	0.6	0.7	0.7
Other consumer goods	3.4	3.1	2.5	2.7	2.8	2.8	3.5	7.5	8.0	7.8
Total	100.0	100.0	100.0	100.0	100.0	100.0	100.0	100.0	100.0	100.0

Source: Appendix A, Table A-3. For figures on movements of quantity and value based on these same classification schemes, see Table A-3.

and power-generating machinery, with the other subcategories remaining fairly constant. The consumer goods category perhaps presents a more interesting development. Although this category shows a decline in its relative importance in the import bundle, this decline has come wholly from declines in food imports. The import of food declined absolutely over the period and the relative share of food imports fell by more than 60 percent (from the 1961-62 average). The other consumer goods categories all have seen an increase in their share of the import bundle. It seems likely that it is this increase in the importation of consumer goods, caused in part by the 1965 reforms, that has dissipated the 1965 improvement in the balance of trade. This consumer goods increase, contributing to the balance-of-trade deficit, is a direct result of the "freeing" of the import sector. Further reforms, as they relax controls on imports, will cause additional increases in these consumer goods categories.

Having examined the changes in the industrial classification of exports and "use" classifications of imports, we can gather some additional information by examining the "Stage of Production" of the import and export bundle.* Table 7 arrays exports and imports by degree of manufacture. Exports, reflecting the growth in industrial exports, show a substantial increase in the export of "more elaborately transformed articles." This increasing share of the export market has come primarily at the expense of the export of "crude articles" with "simply transformed articles" only slightly losing its relative share of this export market. In the import sector the changes are not so drastic. "More elaborately transformed articles" compose the largest increase in relative share of the import market. "Simply transformed articles" also show an increase, with "crude articles" recording the loss. These data further support the contention that the Yugoslav export sector is emerging from the characteristic pattern of an underdeveloped economy. The export mix is becoming more industrialized and consists of articles increasingly more "transformed." Similarly, these data reflect the trend away from the importation of basic foodstuffs and the increasing industrialization of the economy.

During this period, Yugoslavia experienced a fluctuating geographic distribution of trade. Table 8, which arrays the percentage share in the export bundle by trading groups, reflects this change.

---

*Statistika Spoljne Trgovine, SFR Jugoslavije (Belgrade: Federal Institute for Statistics) presents no explanation of any decision rule used in placing goods in any of the three categories.

TABLE 7

Exports and Imports by Stage of Production, 1960–69
(degree of manufacture)

Stage of Production	Percent of Total									
	1960	1961	1962	1963	1964	1965	1966	1967	1968	1969
Exports										
Crude articles	25.7	24.7	19.6	20.8	17.1	12.5	13.4	15.9	14.1	12.5
Simply transformed articles	38.7	38.4	37.6	36.7	38.5	33.5	33.2	31.5	32.0	34.2
More elaborately Transformed articles	35.6	36.9	42.8	42.5	44.4	54.0	53.4	52.6	53.9	53.3
Imports										
Crude articles	20.2	24.2	26.6	30.4	23.6	28.1	24.7	17.7	15.5	16.8
Simply transformed articles	22.7	21.6	22.1	21.8	24.6	23.2	22.7	25.0	22.9	23.1
More elaborately Transformed articles	57.1	54.2	51.3	47.8	51.8	48.7	52.6	57.3	61.6	60.1

Source: Appendix A, Table A-4. For figures on movements of quantity and value rather than percentage share, see Table A-4.

30

TABLE 8

Exports and Imports by Geographical Area, 1960-69

Exports and Imports by Trading Group	Percent of Total											
	1950	1955	1960	1961	1962	1963	1964	1965	1966	1967	1968	1969
Exports												
Comecon[a]	34.5	13.6	32.0	30.7	24.0	26.7	34.5	41.8	36.2	35.4	33.0	29.1
EEC	36.4	35.1	25.2	25.6	26.5	33.2	27.2	25.1	27.5	29.7	28.9	33.0
EFTA		20.3	16.4	15.9	15.4	14.7	13.6	9.6	11.5	11.7	13.0	14.2
U.S.	13.5	10.6	5.7	6.9	8.7	6.5	6.2	6.1	6.5	6.3	7.3	6.3
Total West[b]	84.4	66.0	47.3	48.3	50.6	54.4	47.0	40.9	45.5	47.6	49.3	53.4
Selected LDC[c]	12.0	18.5	17.2	19.8	24.6	18.0	17.3	16.3	16.9	14.0	16.2	13.7
Imports												
Comecon	35.6	7.2	25.9	18.9	21.4	22.6	28.7	28.7	31.2	25.5	27.2	23.9
EEC	29.6	29.6	33.0	36.7	28.8	27.5	28.5	26.1	26.3	40.0	39.3	39.4
EFTA	29.6	17.3	16.3	15.0	14.0	13.9	12.4	13.1	13.5	15.3	16.3	18.8
U.S.	21.5	33.0	17.3	19.7	20.6	17.7	13.0	15.2	12.7	7.4	5.1	4.2
Total West	86.7	79.9	66.7	71.3	63.3	59.1	53.9	54.3	52.5	62.7	60.7	62.3
Selected LDC	12.2	9.7	11.2	8.8	12.7	13.4	14.0	13.0	12.0	11.7	10.3	13.4

[a]Includes Albania for all years.
[b]EEC, EFTA, and U.S.
[c]Less developed countries. For list of countries, see Appendix A, Table A-5.

Source: Appendix A, Tables A-5 and A-6.

Exports to the bloc countries reached a peak in 1965, accounting for
almost 42 percent of Yugoslavia's exports. Since 1965, the relative
share of exports to the bloc has decreased annually with all subsequent
years recording an absolute level below the 1965 peak. This dramatic
increase in exports to the bloc had the most pronounced effect on exports to the EFTA countries. All the EFTA countries showed a decline
in their relative share of the Yugoslav export market, with Austria
and the United Kingdom recording an absolute decline. Since 1965,
the trend has been reversed. In the late 1960s, exports to the West
accounted for an increasing share of the export sector; this increase
in relative share is evident in both the EEC and EFTA, with the EEC
replacing Comecon (in 1969) as Yugoslavia's primary export market.

Imports present a similar pattern. The peak in imports from
the bloc countries came in 1966, one year later than the export peak.
Although Yugoslavia increased its purchases from the bloc countries
in every year after 1966, these purchases represented a declining
share of total imports. As in exports, the EEC countries represent
the primary market for Yugoslav imports.

This section has described changes in the international trade
sector of Yugoslavia. In summary, the following points are mentioned.
Trade turnover measured on a per capita basis has increased to a level
above that calculated for other less developed countries. The trade
balance showed signs of improving in 1965, but has deteriorated in
every subsequent year. The bundle of traded goods has also changed.
Exports have become increasingly more industrial, while importation
of reproduction goods has become more important. In both imports
and exports, the trend has been toward "more elaborately transformed"
articles. The direction of this trade has also undergone changes. A
trend in the early 1960s toward increased participation in Comecon
reached a peak in 1965-66 and reversed itself in the last three years
of the decade.

                            TRADE WITH COMECON

In 1954, Yugoslavia resumed trading with the Comecon countries.
This resumption ended the five-year (1949-54) blockade that had forced
Yugoslavia to look westward. By 1956, Yugoslavia had reconciled with
Comecon and was admitted to observer status, which she still holds
today. As we saw above, Comecon trade reached a peak in 1965-66
and has been declining in relative importance in recent years. In

this section we will examine trends in Yugoslavia's participation in
Comecon.*

The incentives for participating in the Comecon organization
quite probably vary among the countries involved. A primary stimulus
behind the Soviet effort is presumably political. The USSR is seeking
stability through the formation of a strong communist commonwealth.
Yugoslavia and the other small Eastern European countries are more
likely to be reacting to economic motives.

> From what followed CEMA's Fourth Meeting, one may in-
> fer that the initiative for promoting "socialist division of
> labor" emanated chiefly from the Eastern Europeans, and
> that the USSR itself displayed very little drive to imple-
> ment the ambitious decision of CEMA. This attitude re-
> flected, in part, the fact that the USSR, then as well as
> later, had no intention of "dividing labor" to the point of
> making itself significantly dependent on outside sources
> of supply in any major branch of heavy industry, and
> generally held that systematic "division of labor was a
> precept whose utility was confined mainly to the smaller
> nations of the Bloc."[6]

Regardless of the motivation, integration has not been as rapid as in
the EEC or the EFTA. Intra-Comecon trade has increased, but this
increase has been at about the same rate as increases in industrial
output, while trade has increased faster than industrial output in both
the EEC and EFTA. Egon Neuberger presents several explanations
for this slow progress.[7] The most convincing of these are the attempt
of each country to protect its national sovereignty, the strong vested
interest in nationalized industries, and the need (in a planned economy)
to take active steps to increase trade, rather than just doing away
with trade barriers. In the instance of the vested interests of the
nationalized industries, integration is slowed by these sectors resisting
any action which would degrade their position or potential position.
The need for the government to take active steps further complicates
integration in light of these interest groups.

---

*It is not the purpose here to examine the intent, history, and
success of Comecon, but rather to view Yugoslavia's experience in
bloc trade. For an excellent history and discussion of the current
problems of Comecon, see Michael Kaser, Comecon (London: Oxford
University Press, 1967).

For example, an agreement on a division of labor that requires the abandonment of the East German Shipbuilding industry in favor of the more efficient Polish industry might be expected to be more difficult than an agreement to lower tariffs and eliminate subsidies on completed ships in all member countries, even though both might have the same end result.[3]

In the case of Yugoslavia, the first reason—national sovereignty— perhaps best explains Yugoslavia's slow integration into bloc trade. Not only does Yugoslavia fiercely guard her national sovereignty but also she has experienced economic sanctions at the lead of the USSR. Fear of infringement on her sovereignty, reinforced by the Czechoslovak invasion, may partially explain the reversal of the early 1960s trend toward greater participation in bloc trade.

Table 9 shows that Yugoslavia's contribution to the total Comecon participation in world trade exceeds her contribution to the total GDP of these same countries. While Yugoslavia accounted for only 2 percent of the Comecon GDP in 1965, her contribution to bloc world imports and exports was 6.2 percent and 5.3 percent, respectively.*

Turning to intrabloc trade, we are confronted with countervailing forces. There are the forces discussed above working to impede integration into the bloc, while the bias of the Yugoslav plant manager, who finds trading within the bloc much to his liking, works against integration. Sales to bloc countries, being planned, are more certain and, more importantly, do not require modern marketing techniques, which are a necessary part of "competing" for sales in Western nations.

Yugoslavia's trade with Comecon is carried out on a different basis than trade with the West. The prereform planning infrastructure

---

*These figures are heavily weighted by the inclusion of the USSR, which accounts for a large amount of total GDP without a proportionate amount of world trade. However, if we compare Yugoslavia's participation in world trade to the East European members of Comecon, we still find Yugoslavia's relative contribution to trade exceeding her relative contribution to GDP (Table 9). These figures are presented to develop Yugoslavia's relative position among the bloc countries. The measure is subject to all the weaknesses discussed in Chapter 2 (see footnote on page 14).

TABLE 9

Yugoslav Participation in Bloc World Trade, 1965 and 1967
(millions of U.S. $)

Country	GDP 1965	Imports 1965	Imports 1967	Exports 1965	Exports 1967
Albania	345				
Bulgaria	5,200	1,178	1,572	1,176	1,458
Czechoslovakia	18,400	2,673	2,680	2,689	2,864
E. Germany	21,700	2,546	2,972	2,776	3,159
Hungary	9,500	1,521	1,776	1,510	1,702
Poland	25,600	2,340	2,645	2,228	2,527
Rumania	11,800	1,077	1,546	1,102	1,395
USSR	265,200	8,058	8,536	8,175	9,649
Yugoslavia	7,240	1,288	1,707	1,092	1,252
Eastern Europe	99,785	12,623	14,898	12,573	14,357
Eastern Europe and USSR	364,985	20,681	23,444	20,748	24,006
Yugoslavia as a percent of total Eastern Europe	7.3	10.2	11.5	8.7	8.7
Yugoslavia as a percent of total Eastern Europe and USSR	2.0	6.2	7.3	5.3	5.2

Source: Appendix A, Tables A-1 and A-7. For Yugoslav participation covering more years, see Table A-7.

remains operational for trade with the Comecon countries.* This
planned or "quasi-planned" trade is bilateral. (There have been two
attempts at multilateral clearing within Comecon. The first, originating in Warsaw in 1957, never became significant. It cleared only
1.5 percent of intra-Comecon trade during its six-year life. The
second agreement, ratified in 1963, proposes to aid in the development
of East-West trade. This second program has not yet developed, with
the all-important Soviet position unknown. As Kaser reports, "gradual
introduction of convertibility was unofficially indicated by Bogomolow
in Komm., no. 18, 1966.")9

        The balance of trade with each East European trade partner
becomes important with such projected bilateralism. These trade
balances may affect the negotiations concerning the next exchange of
products. It is, therefore, important to examine Yugoslavia's balance
of trade with each of the Comecon countries (see Table 10). These
balances are consistently negative, with the Comecon trading partners
running surpluses with Yugoslavia. The glaring exception is the case
of the Soviet Union. Poland in the early 1960s also presents an exception; this surplus may explain the declining trend in Yugoslav-Polish
trade. The direction of Yugoslav trade with the Comecon countries
may be influenced by these trade balances. A positive trade balance
(a surplus) indicates that Yugoslavia is granting credits; a negative
balance (a deficit) indicates she is receiving credits. Yugoslavia, an
underdeveloped country herself, is financing the development of the
Soviet Union by running a consistent surplus in her trade balance.**
This surplus with the USSR might be viewed as a cost of "being allowed"
to participate in intra-Comecon trade. Since 1967 (the peak year for
both the Soviet Union's share of Yugoslav exports and the Yugoslav
surplus), there has been a trend away from increased exports to the
USSR. If we can regard the trade balance surplus with the Soviet
Union as a "price" Yugoslavia must pay for "favorable relations" and
consequent access to bloc markets, the decreased surplus may be
evidence of increased independence on the part of Yugoslavia.

————————————

        *This dichotomy in methods of trading will be discussed in
greater detail in Chapter 4, and the consequences examined in subsequent chapters.

        **Yugoslavia's consistent deficits with the Satellite countries
would then indicate the financing of Yugoslavia's development.

TABLE 10

Yugoslavia's Trade Balance with
Comecon Countries, 1960-69

Trade Balance
(Value in thousands of new dinars)

Country	1960	1961	1962	1963	1964	1965	1966	1967	1968	1969	1960-69
Albania	-3,465	-948	-990	-6,476	-9,729	989	-1,746	9,990	-19,061	2,793	-28,643
Bulgaria	-15,427	-48,922	-72,353	-19,181	-104,981	-89,965	-282,560	120	258	-90,472	-723,483
Czechoslovakia	-6,971	-33,578	-55,440	-247,417	-456,451	-2,135	-340,715	-558,845	-604,422	-736,580	-3,042,354
E. Germany	93,513	-131,959	-28,586	-137,197	-117,763	156,033	-303,628	-74,264	-233,068	-466,209	-1,243,128
Hungary	-207,900	-187,110	-123,503	-167,887	-147,588	-49,583	-48,166	-41,896	-75,405	793	-1,048,205
Poland	-198,948	146,437	126,266	61,999	-248,953	89,445	-196,734	54,422	-95,781	-7,055	-268,902
Rumania	-48,840	34,732	44,220	-19,181	-3,887	-39,584	-51,668	23,949	8,745	-35,067	-86,581
USSR	-26,647	252,243	-186,656	185,666	205,779	1,000,383	617,446	682,719	114,438	315,741	3,161,112
Total Comecon	-414,662	30,896	-297,041	-349,717	-883,573	1,065,623	-607,771	96,389	-904,296	-1,016,056	-3,280,208

Source: Appendix A, Table A-7.

Table 11 arrays the country's share of Yugoslav's trade with
the Comecon countries. The USSR enjoyed an increasing share (after
the 1955 high) of the Yugoslav exports and imports, reaching a high
for the decade in 1967-68. The turnabout during the decade is substantial. Poland, second only to the Soviet Union, begins the period
accounting for approximately a quarter of Yugoslavia's bloc exports.
This share declines with fluctuations throughout the entire decade.
The relative importance of East Germany diminishes substantially
during the 1960s. East Germany begins the decade as a primary
source of imports for the Yugoslavs and their third most important
import-export market. By 1969, the Soviet Union and Czechoslovakia
both account for larger portions of Yugoslavia's imports from the
bloc, East Germany has slipped to fifth in relative importance as a
market for Yugoslav exports. In general, the period 1960-69 shows
Albania, Czechoslovakia, and the Soviet Union accounting for an increased share of Yugoslav exports. Poland and East Germany account
for the declines, with the rest of the bloc countries maintaining their
positions. Imports reflect this same trend, with Albania, Czechoslovakia, and the USSR registering increases in their share of the
Yugoslavia import market. Hungary, Poland, and East Germany
record losses in the bloc share of Yugoslav imports.

In this section we have looked with greater detail into Yugoslavia's international trading relations with the bloc countries. Several
important points emerged. Yugoslavia, when grouped with Comecon,
accounted for a disproportionate share (based on GDP) of the group's
participation in world imports and exports. Intrabloc trade, which
was an increasing share of Yugoslavia's total trade in 1960-66, has
since declined. Within this bloc trade there have been substantial
shifts in market share with the USSR, Albania, and Czechoslovakia
increasing their percentages throughout the period of the 1960s.
Finally, Yugoslavia has run a consistent balance-of-trade surplus
with the Soviet Union and deficit with the other Comecon members.

TRADE WITH THE WEST

Trade with Western Europe and the United States, stimulated
by the hostile action of the early postwar Stalinist regimes, has continued to be the primary source of Yugoslav imports and market for
exports. Throughout the decade of the 1960s, the "West" (EEC, EFTA,
and the U.S.) has accounted for approximately 50 percent of Yugoslavia's exports and over 60 percent of her imports.* This trade with

---

*See Table 8.

TABLE 11

Direction of Yugoslav-Comecon Trade,
1955, 1960-69

Country	1955	1960	1961	1962	1963	1964	1965	1966	1967	1968	1969
Exports											
Albania	0.6	0.2	0.1	0.3	0.1	0.3	0.4	0.4	0.6	0.3	0.7
Bulgaria	1.6	5.1	4.6	3.4	4.2	3.2	3.8	2.9	3.7	6.2	4.2
Czechoslovakia	20.1	14.1	9.7	12.7	11.0	14.5	15.6	15.3	11.2	13.0	14.5
E. Germany	5.3	24.8	15.4	20.5	17.8	20.5	16.6	14.5	14.1	12.8	9.5
Hungary	7.5	11.1	10.2	6.6	5.8	7.7	5.7	6.6	6.1	6.8	10.1
Poland	11.0	12.1	23.2	25.5	18.1	12.8	14.1	12.7	10.3	8.7	10.9
Rumania	2.4	2.4	6.0	4.3	2.3	3.2	2.8	3.8	5.0	5.0	4.9
USSR	51.5	30.2	30.9	26.7	40.6	37.7	41.1	43.8	48.9	46.9	45.2
Imports											
Albania	0.0	0.3	0.1	0.3	0.3	0.4	0.5	0.4	0.4	0.6	0.5
Bulgaria	4.1	4.8	6.9	6.1	4.4	4.8	6.6	7.2	3.8	5.3	4.9
Czechoslovakia	19.6	12.1	11.4	13.5	18.1	21.4	19.2	19.3	21.7	21.0	23.7
E. Germany	6.6	17.4	21.9	19.1	20.4	19.2	17.1	18.0	15.7	14.7	15.3
Hungary	8.7	17.2	19.1	11.0	10.8	9.4	8.0	6.7	6.9	7.0	8.5
Poland	13.2	17.7	16.7	16.9	13.9	15.7	15.4	14.7	9.5	9.1	9.3
Rumania	1.8	3.9	4.4	1.9	2.7	2.7	4.3	4.2	4.7	4.1	4.7
USSR	45.9	26.5	19.4	31.2	29.5	26.4	28.9	29.3	37.2	38.1	33.0

Source: Appendix A, Tables A-5 and A-6.

the West has had several effects on the Yugoslav economy. Most
importantly, it enabled Yugoslavia to survive the Stalinist attacks
manifested in the economic blockade. The fear of Soviet military in-
tervention brought Western military and economic assistance, particularly from the United States. (From 1946 to 1966, Yugoslavia received
$3,668,300,000 [after repayments and interest] in military and economic
assistance from the United States. About 25 percent of this aid was
military assistance and about 40 percent consisted of Food for Peace
grants.)[10] This aid allowed Yugoslavia to use her scarce capital
reserves for economic projects. Another important and often neglected
aspect of the Comecon blockade and the resulting Western assistance
is the opening of Yugoslavia to Western ideas, information, and
technology. In addition to moderating the Yugoslav economic con-
ditions, the foreign aid opened information channels. A barrage of
Western news, cultural material, and technical aid accompanied the
economic and military assistance. These flows of facts and ideas
have, no doubt, had an effect on Yugoslav policies and may be a
contributing factor to the "liberal reforms" and relative "openness"
of Yugoslav society.*

If we include Yugoslavia in the East European bloc, we see that
she accounts for a disproportionate share of bloc trade with the West
(see Table 12). In 1965, Yugoslavia accounted for 9.2 percent of the
bloc exports to Western Europe and 13.7 percent of imports from
Western Europe, while accounting for only 2 percent of the GDP of
the Comecon countries. Furthermore, Yugoslavia's share of bloc
participation in Western Europe increased in the latter part of the
decade. This increased involvement in the markets of Western Europe
has not been proportional, as reflected in figures showing the direction of Yugoslav-Western Europe trade. Dividing Yugoslav trade
with Western markets into the three major trading groups (EFTA,
EEC, U.S.), we see that the direction of Yugoslav trade with the West,
while remaining fairly stable as a percentage of the total, has undergone some geographical changes (see Table 13). The most significant
changes occur in the origin of imports. Throughout the decade,
Yugoslavia's imports from the United States declined. ** This decline

---

*While it is impossible to quantify the effect of this "information"
on Yugoslav policy, the fact is that Yugoslavia is the most "open"
of the socialist republics.

**Yugoslav imports from the U.S. decline relatively throughout
the decade and absolutely after 1966.

TABLE 12

Yugoslav Participation in Bloc Trade with
Western Europe, 1960, 1965, and 1967
(millions of U.S. $)

From:	Exports to Western Europe		
	1960	1965	1967
Eastern Europe*	2,320	3,690	4,540
Yugoslavia	255	373	564
Yugoslavia's percent Participation	9.9	9.2	11.1

To:	Imports from Western Europe		
Eastern Europe	2,130	3,310	4,370
Yugoslavia	396	527	905
Yugoslavia's percent participation	15.7	13.7	17.2

*Albania, Bulgaria, Czechoslovakia, East Germany, Hungary, Poland, Rumania, and USSR. Transactions between East and West Germany are omitted.

Source: Organization for Economic Cooperation and Development, Yugoslavia, OECD Economic Surveys (Geneva, Switzerland: OECD, 1969), p. 51; United Nations Statistical Yearbook, (New York: United Nations, 1969), pp. 398-405.

in relative share, from a high of 32.5 percent in 1962 to 6.6 percent in 1969, reflects decreases in US economic assistance to Yugoslavia. (The high share of U.S. exports in Yugoslavia's import bundle in the 1950s and early 1960s reflects the large amounts of tied economic aid and other such assistance. The large decline has come in large part from the decline in wheat. In 1963, 48.8 percent of Yugoslavia's imports from the U.S. consisted of one item, unmilled wheat. In 1969 Yugoslavia imported no unmilled wheat from the U.S.)[11] This substantial decrease in the share of U.S. participation is offset by increased imports from both the EFTA and the EEC. At the end of the 1960s, well over 60 percent of Yugoslavia's imports from Western markets (39.4 percent of total imports) were from countries of the EEC.

TABLE 13

Direction of Yugoslav Trade with Western Markets,
1950, 1955, 1960-69

Country						Share of Market						
	1950	1955	1960	1961	1962	1963	1964	1965	1966	1967	1968	1969
Exports												
U.S.	16.0	16.0	12.1	14.3	17.1	11.9	13.1	15.1	14.3	13.2	14.8	11.6
EFTA	43.0	30.7	34.7	32.8	30.5	27.1	28.9	23.4	25.2	24.5	26.4	26.5
Austria	12.7	9.0	11.4	9.7	8.1	6.7	7.3	5.8	7.1	7.2	7.0	5.8
Denmark	0.7	0.5	0.6	0.7	0.6	0.8	1.2	0.9	0.7	0.6	0.7	0.7
Portugal	0.0	0.0	0.0	0.0	0.0	0.0	0.0	0.0	0.0	0.0	0.0	0.0
Sweden	2.9	0.8	1.8	2.1	1.8	2.7	1.9	2.0	2.6	2.0	2.7	2.1
Switzerland	4.7	7.9	3.2	2.8	5.7	3.6	4.4	4.8	6.2	6.4	6.0	6.5
UK	22.8	12.5	17.8	17.5	14.2	13.2	14.1	9.9	8.6	8.3	10.0	11.3
EEC	40.9	53.3	53.1	52.9	52.3	61.0	58.0	61.4	60.5	62.3	58.7	61.9
Belgium-Luxembourg	3.6	1.5	1.7	1.7	1.3	1.0	1.4	1.6	1.6	1.4	1.7	1.5
France	4.1	5.4	3.2	3.5	2.8	4.1	4.5	4.0	5.2	4.7	4.6	5.5
Netherlands	4.6	3.9	2.2	2.1	1.6	1.6	2.3	2.4	2.8	2.5	2.7	2.8
Italy	13.9	23.2	27.8	25.5	27.2	36.6	31.5	32.7	31.2	38.1	30.2	31.4
W. Germany	14.7	19.3	18.1	20.1	19.3	17.8	18.3	20.8	19.7	15.7	19.4	20.7
Total	100.0	100.0	100.0	100.0	100.0	100.0	100.0	100.0	100.0	100.0	100.0	100.0
Imports												
U.S.	24.8	41.3	26.0	27.5	32.5	29.9	24.2	28.0	24.2	11.8	8.4	6.6
EFTA	34.2	21.7	24.5	21.1	22.1	23.5	23.0	24.0	25.7	24.4	26.8	30.0
Austria	8.8	5.4	6.7	4.9	5.7	5.4	4.9	4.9	5.0	6.0	7.7	8.0
Denmark	0.4	0.4	0.9	0.9	0.4	0.8	0.6	0.9	0.4	0.5	0.6	0.6
Portugal	0.0	0.0	0.0	0.0	0.0	0.0	0.0	0.0	0.0	0.0	0.0	0.0
Sweden	1.6	1.1	1.6	1.5	1.8	2.1	2.3	2.1	1.5	1.7	1.9	2.3
Switzerland	4.0	3.9	3.5	3.7	3.0	3.8	3.6	3.5	4.3	4.7	6.0	7.5
U.K.	19.4	11.0	11.9	10.1	11.2	11.3	11.7	12.7	14.4	11.4	10.7	11.7
EEC	41.0	37.0	49.4	51.4	45.7	46.6	52.8	48.0	50.1	63.8	64.7	63.3
Belgium-Luxembourg	2.0	1.7	1.8	2.2	1.5	1.6	1.8	1.7	2.1	3.0	1.8	1.6
France	3.4	3.4	5.4	3.7	4.9	7.8	7.2	7.0	5.7	8.0	6.1	5.5
Netherlands	4.7	3.6	3.4	3.1	2.7	3.3	3.8	3.2	2.9	3.2	2.8	2.9
Italy	12.0	12.4	17.0	20.5	18.4	18.2	24.4	19.7	20.5	21.8	24.6	24.0
W. Germany	19.0	15.9	21.8	22.0	18.0	15.7	15.6	16.4	19.0	27.9	29.5	29.3
Total	100.0	100.0	100.0	100.0	100.0	100.0	100.0	100.0	100.0	100.0	100.0	100.0

Source: Appendix A, Tables A-5 and A-6.

Export markets present a somewhat different picture. The geographic distribution of Yugoslavia's exports is quite stable. There are slight yearly fluctuations in the country share, but the pattern is relatively stable.

The country distribution of trade reflects the group pattern. On the export side, the relative position of each country is quite stable. At the beginning of the decade, Italy (27.8 percent), West Germany (18.1 percent), U.K. (17.8 percent), and the U.S. (12.1 percent) account for the bulk of Yugoslavia's exports to the West. Next in importance we find Austria, France, and Switzerland. In 1969, the order has changed little. The United States has replaced the U.K. as the third most important Western buyer, but the four still account for the majority of Yugoslavia's sales (about 75 percent). In the second group, Switzerland has moved ahead of both Austria and France as a purchaser of Yugoslav goods. On the import side, there are more significant changes caused by the substantial decline in the purchase of U.S. goods. In 1960, the U.S. is the most important source of imports, accounting for 26 percent of Yugoslavia's imports from Western markets. West Germany (21.8 percent), Italy (17.5 percent), and the U.K. (11.9 percent) again complete the important group of Yugoslavia's sources of imports. By the end of the decade, there has been considerable change, with West Germany, Italy, and the U.K. all increasing in importance. In addition, both Austria and Switzerland have captured a larger share of the Yugoslav market than the United States.

What of the future of Yugoslavia's trade with the West? It was pointed out earlier that the mid-1960s saw a relative slump in Yugoslavia's trade with the West, but that, in the latter half of the decade, increases were evident. Can we expect the trend toward Western integration to continue? There are several contradicting forces at work. On the side of increased integration, we should place Yugoslavia's unique position.

In the context of this discussion, we will concern ourselves with U.S.-Yugoslav relations and use these as an indication of the "Western" position. Although the U.S. share of the Yugoslav market is declining, the U.S. commercial position and influence in Western Europe make her position more important. As Pisar points out,

Wholly foreign firms, too, particularly those substantially involved in the US market, have been known to decline or camouflage legitimate transactions with the East for fear of displeasing their American clients. Occasionally, such firms have been victims of attitudes adopted by

their governments. This was demonstrated by the angry
American reactions to Sweden's persistent harboring of
deserters from the Vietnam war and the announcement
in October 1969, of a proposed $40 million grant to Hanoi.
Prices fell in the Stockholm stock exchange, especially
those of large and vulnerable companies such as Volvo
(automobiles) and Stora Kopparbug (mining). The latter
was reported to have lost 33.6 million in cancelled
orders.[12]

Yugoslavia has experienced a long history of preferential treatment from the United States. This dates to the Trade Agreements
Extension Act of 1951, and the Trade Expansion Act of 1962, which
withdrew most-favored nation (MFN) treatment from goods originating
in East Europe. The 1951 act excluded Yugoslavia, and, in 1963,
an amendment to the 1962 act was passed which enabled the President
to extend nondiscriminatory treatment to Yugoslavia in order to pro-
mote independence and prevent "domination or control (of Yugoslavia)
by international communism."[13] The U.S. has a history of extending
MFN treatment to Yugoslavia, but the stigma of "trading with the
enemy" persists. As an example, in 1965, letters of approval from
the Department of State, Defense, and Commerce were solicited (to
be used in the event of public controversy) before the major cigarette
companies imported Yugoslav tobacco.[14] (Such fears on the part of
businessmen are probably more acute in dealings with other communist
countries, but are also a part of transactions with Yugoslavia.) Two
very strong forces are evident: one promoting trade to "free" Yugoslavia, the other opposing trade on the grounds "we cannot both feed
and fight communism." A recent Commerce Department publication
recommends the Yugoslav market to U.S. businessmen, predicting
good markets for electronic equipment and equipment for the tourist,
agriculture, and food-processing industries.[15]

The tourist industry presents another possibility for Yugoslavia
to earn hard currency and thereby integrate more fully into Western
markets. Continuous liberalization of border and customs formalities,
complemented by investment in tourist facilities, has increased the
tourist market. The tourist industry grew from a contributor of
$40.2 billion in foreign exchange earnings in 1962 to $150 billion in
1966.[16] (Austria and West Germany account for 45.5 percent of these
tourist exports, measured by tourist nights by country of origin.)

In reviewing prospects for future growth in Yugoslav trade with
the West, we must re-emphasize the history of preferential treatment
for Yugoslavia and the outright support of the U.S. Government in

encouraging firms to engage in trade with the East. The emotional issue, however, still exists. The apprehension on the part of some Western businessmen caused by this cold war stigma, coupled with the lack of experience in marketing techniques on the part of Yugoslav entrepreneurs, will work to slow the increased integration anticipated by reformers.

TRADE WITH THE DEVELOPING COUNTRIES

The underdeveloped countries hold a small share of Yugoslavia's present trade package but are looked upon as an area of tremendous opportunity for growth. These countries can supply raw materials and are a natural outlet for Yugoslavia's industrial output. A Yugoslav source, quoted by Carole Sawyer, notes that

> While industrially developed Western countries consider the finished products of Yugoslav industry with some reservations, especially concerning machines, metal construction, means of transportation, etc., these products have more favorable placement conditions . . . especially in certain Asian, African, and Latin American countries.[17]

However appealing this trade with the underdeveloped nations may be, it presents an added problem. This trade, often linked with economic aid, would imply that Yugoslavia, an underdeveloped country herself, would be passing on a part of the aid she receives.

In his book on Soviet foreign aid, Goldman presents three reasons for Soviet aid and trade: the economic, the desire to maintain and expand trade relations; the humanitarian, the desire to aid those poorer than themselves, those who have "been plundered by the imperialists"; and the political, "whether or not an action will advance the (political) interests of the USSR."[18] Examining Yugoslavia's economic assistance, it would appear that Goldman's first reason is overwhelmingly dominant. Yugoslavia has little to gain by political propaganda and is too poor herself to "afford" international humanitarianism. It seems likely that any economic assistance granted by Yugoslavia is motivated by a desire to expand economic relations with the recipient country. To the extent that trade with these underdeveloped countries is bilateral, the balance of trade might indicate the granting or receiving of credits. These credits could indicate the granting of economic assistance to some countries and the receipt of it from those with whom Yugoslavia runs a balance-of-trade

deficit. Further implications demand more complete analysis, and
are beyond the scope of this investigation. (See Appendix A, Tables
A-5 and A-6. See Figure 1, infra, for a list of underdeveloped countries with which Yugoslavia has bilateral agreements.)

Despite all the claims of increased activity in trade with developing countries, this growth has not come about. The 1960s records a
slight decline in the relative share of exports to this group and a
fairly stable level of imports from them. Yugoslavia is, however,
the most active Comecon participant in trade with developing nations.
In 1964, Yugoslavia conducted a larger share of her trade with the
underdeveloped countries than any of the other bloc nations (see Table
14). The largest share of this trade with the underdeveloped countries
was with the countries of Asia and the Middle East. In 1969, 78 percent
of Yugoslavia's exports to the developing countries, and 67 percent
of her imports from them, were transacted with countries of Asia
and the Middle East (see Table 15). Examining this trade by country,
we find that a substantial share of it is carried out with relatively
few countries. For example, in 1969, 46 percent of Yugoslavia's
exports to developing countries consisted of exports to three countries:
Greece, India, and the UAR. These same countries accounted for 43
percent of Yugoslavia's imports from the underdeveloped world.
Iran, Pakistan, and Israel round out the group of significant export

TABLE 14

Share of Developing Countries in Total Foreign
Trade Turnover of Bloc Countries, 1964

Country	Percent
Yugoslavia	14.6
Soviet Union	10.3
Czechoslovakia	9.0
Poland	7.7
Hungary (1963)	6.4
Bulgaria	5.0
Rumania	5.0
East Germany	3.8

Source: Kurt Muller, The Foreign Aid Programs of the Soviet
Bloc and Communist China, trans. R. H. Walker and Michael Roloff
(New York: Walker, 1967), p. 144.

TABLE 15

Percent Share by Area in International Trade of Yugoslavia
with Developing Countries, 1950, 1955, 1960-69

Area	Year											
	1950	1955	1960	1961	1962	1963	1964	1965	1966	1967	1968	1969
Exports												
Africa	3.1	5.9	6.9	6.4	13.7	21.9	14.3	15.6	13.1	8.9	7.2	12.1
Asia	1.0	1.7	26.8	34.8	36.6	32.2	37.1	39.8	36.7	28.5	32.0	30.8
Europe	0.0	0.0	1.4	1.8	0.8	0.9	1.6	1.2	1.1	1.5	4.1	3.0
Latin and South America	49.8	34.7	9.8	10.5	18.3	11.2	13.9	5.4	7.3	10.6	8.1	6.9
Middle East	46.1	57.7	55.2	46.4	30.6	33.7	33.1	37.9	41.9	50.5	48.6	47.2
Imports												
Africa	0.3	0.1	6.2	8.4	8.6	14.9	16.8	15.0	11.6	10.0	12.1	10.6
Asia	2.8	5.8	19.7	20.4	29.1	30.2	22.5	22.4	19.4	19.6	20.3	22.6
Europe	0.0	0.0	2.3	4.1	2.5	0.6	1.2	2.4	3.3	1.8	3.8	6.3
Latin and South America	55.5	40.5	13.0	23.6	15.3	19.2	26.7	23.1	28.4	25.6	21.7	16.0
Middle East	41.4	53.6	58.9	43.2	44.5	35.0	32.7	37.1	38.7	42.9	42.0	44.4

Source: Appendix A, Tables A-5 and A-6. The same country classification scheme that was employed
by Carole A. Sawyer, Communist Trade with the Developing Countries: 1955-65 (New York: Praeger, 1966),
is used.

markets in 1969. In imports, Pakistan, Malaysia, Iraq, Iran, and
Brazil constitute the important relative share by 1969.* This pattern
of concentrated trade with a relatively few underdeveloped countries
is characteristic of Comecon trade with the developing countries.[19]
Yugoslavia, while conforming to the Comecon pattern, seems to be
more involved with a greater number of countries.**

Perhaps the most striking feature about the direction of this
trade, when compared to Yugoslav trade with either the Comecon or
Western trade, is its instability. Each country's share in this trade
goes through considerable changes throughout the decade. In large
measure, this reflects the smaller absolute bundle of goods traded
and the effect single large sales or purchases would have on relative
share (see Tables A-5 and A-6).

The commodity composition of Yugoslav trade with developing
countries conforms to the pattern of the other Communist countries.
A substantial share (almost 80 percent) of purchases from these
countries consists of crude materials and food products.[20] Although
not comprising a significant share, Yugoslavia does provide a market
for manufactured goods from the developing countries. These purchases will likely increase, following the general Yugoslav pattern of
increased importation of manufactured products.

A TRADE PATTERN

In summarizing the results of this statistical inquiry, we have
examined Yugoslavia's foreign trade experience through the decade.
The pattern that appears is consistent with the observation that
Yugoslavia is emerging from underdeveloped status. The exports
come increasingly from the industrial sector and the export bundle
is increasingly "transformed." Imports consist more of reproduction
and consumption (other than food) goods. As the development process
continues, Yugoslavia has become more involved in foreign trade than
the Comecon countries. This trading activity has not yet, however,
approached the levels of that in the West European countries.

---

*See Appendix A, Tables A-5 and A-6.

**Yugoslavia reports trade with more than forty developing
countries (see Appendix A).

The geographic pattern of Yugoslav trade has undergone some changes during the decade. In the first half of the decade, Yugoslavia became increasingly involved in Comecon. This trend reached a high for the decade in 1965-66. Total trade with the underdeveloped countries of the world has remained fairly stable (despite claims to the contrary) throughout the decade. Within the three groups discussed, there have also been some geographic changes. These changes seem to reflect trade orientation based more on economic parameters, than on political or economic aid criteria.*

Predicting the future is quite dangerous, and doubly so when the sociopolitical climate is unstable. Given no abrupt change in policy, the pattern does suggest that we can expect Yugoslavia to become more involved in the world market. It is safe to expect the export bundle to continue to become more industrialized as Yugoslavia continues her industrial development. As Yugoslavia progresses on her "own road to socialism," and as the reforms become more operational, the direction of Yugoslavia's trade should turn more toward the EEC and the underdeveloped markets.

NOTES

1. H. G. Shaffer, "Yugoslavia's Own Road to Socialism: A Non-Marxist View," in H. G. Shaffer, ed., The Communist World: Marxist and Non-Marxist Views (New York: Appleton-Century-Crofts, 1967), p. 224.

2. Secretariat of the Economic Commission for Europe, The European Economy in 1965, United Nations, p. 64.

3. Ljubisa S. Adamovich, "Economic Reform in Foreign Trade in Eastern Europe," Grado Seminar, Italy (Thomas Jefferson Center, University of Virginia and CESES, Milan, Italy, August 1970; mimeographed).

4. H. G. Shaffer, "Yugoslavia's 'Own Road to Socialism': A Non-Marxist View," p. 241.

5. H. Leibenstein, Economic Backwardness and Economic Growth (New York: John Wiley and Sons, 1957), p. 40.

---

*The large dependence on U.S. imports was a result of economic aid for political reasons.

6. Oleg Hoeffding, Recent Efforts Toward Coordinated Economic Planning in the Soviet Bloc, P-1768 (Santa Monica, Calif.: The RAND Corporation, August 1959), p. 5.

7. Egon Neuberger, Soviet Economic Integration: Some Suggested Explanations for Slow Progress, RM 3629 (Santa Monica, Calif.: The RAND Corporation, July 1963).

8. Ibid., p. 15.

9. Michael Kaser, Comecon (London: Oxford University Press, 1967), p. 169.

10. S. C. Markovich, "The Influence of American Foreign Aid on Yugoslav Policies, 1948-1966" (unpublished Ph.D. dissertation, University of Virginia, June 1968).

11. Statistika Spoljne Trgovine SFR Jugoslavije, (Belgrade: Federal Institute for Statistics), 1963, p. 317, and 1969, p. 571.

12. Samuel Pisar, Coexistence and Commerce (New York: McGraw-Hill, 1970), p. 86.

13. Ibid., p. 98.

14. Ibid., p. 86.

15. "Market Factors in Yugoslavia," Overseas Business Reports (Washington: U.S. Government Printing Office, May 1969).

16. Milan Mazi, "Tourism 1962-1967," Yugoslav Survey, IX (February 1968), p. 74.

17. Carole A. Sawyer, Communist Trade with Developing Countries: 1955-65 (New York: Praeger, 1966), p. 42.

18. Marshall I. Goldman, Soviet Foreign Aid (New York: Praeger, 1967), pp. 185-89.

19. Kurt Muller, The Foreign Aid Programs of the Soviet Bloc and Communist China, trans. R. H. Weber and Michael Roloff (New York: Walker, 1967); and Carole A. Sawyer, Communist Trade with Developing Countries.

20. Sawyer, Communist Trade with Developing Countries, p. 33.

4

THE REFORM
OF INTERNATIONAL TRADE
AND STATE TRADING

This chapter will outline the goals and consequences of Yugoslavia's recent economic reforms as they relate to international trade in general, and state trading in particular. We will begin with a discussion of the reforms that relate to the foreign trade sector of the economy, followed by an examination of the effect of these reforms on the state trading apparatus in Yugoslavia.

THE REFORM MOVEMENT
AND INTERNATIONAL TRADE

Reform in Yugoslavia has occurred frequently since 1947.[1] The political, social, and economic systems have been changed rapidly, and the constitution has been reorganized frequently. (The Constitution of 1947 was changed with a new Constitutional Law in 1953. This constituted a major revision of the political and economic system. In 1963, there was another revision with some additional corrections in 1967.)[2] These reforms have caught the attention of many Western observers.

As far as economic pragmatism is concerned, Yugoslavia is not only far ahead of any Moscow bloc country, but in fact, is playing the reformist game in quite a different league. While the other countries are still essentially trying to improve the old, traditional system of planning and management, the Yugoslavs are making a real effort to

evolve a workable alternative—an altogether new
system.[3]

The general tenor of the economic reform movement has been the
gradual withdrawal of central state institutions from economic au-
thority. This has been attempted through the rise of workers' self-
management, and the drastic overhaul of the price system, among
other things. In 1963, the New Constitution confirmed, in principle,
the legal framework of decentralized self-government. Then, in
1964, the Eighth Congress of the League of Communists restated
this same policy in political terms. The 1965 reform was, in fact,
the technical application of these principles. Though this 1965 reform
was not as politically glamorous, it was this institutionalizing that
gave substance to the previous "reforms."

One of the major goals of the Economic Reform was the integration of Yugoslavia into the world economy. As envisioned, this
would force Yugoslav enterprises to be more sensitive to the bene-
ficial influences of similar enterprises in developed countries. As
Professor Bicanic, University of Zagreb, pointed out:

> Whether interprises are going concerns must be tested
> on the market. Prices are to be those of the world
> market, and enterprises which cannot stand such com-
> petition, with normal customs' protection, will have
> to make efforts to do so, and reorganize, or close
> their doors.[4]

This argument should not be dismissed as merely an academic
polemic. It was accepted by political leaders. Vladimir Bakaric,
Croatian Communist leader, pushed for such reform. He argued
that, "unless Yugoslavia's enterprises would be able to reach the
level of the world market, they would eventually go out of business."[5]
(In this instance as in other aspects of the reform movement, the
stated intent has not been carried to its conclusion; enterprises have
not been allowed to fail.)

The objectives of the Economic Reform were:

> To ensure a broader integration into the inter-
> national division of labor, increase the volume
> of exports and imports of commodities and
> services, and strengthen Yugoslavia's economic
> relations with other countries,

      To base external trade on dinar earnings and
to abolish budget subsidies for exports paid in the
form of premiums and other special incentives,

      To ensure a greater influence of the foreign
market and the more developed economies on the
national economy, its business criteria, and con-
ditions of operation,

      To liberalize external trade and payments
traffic,

      To level off the balance of payments with all
areas, especially with hard currency countries,

      To achieve the convertibility of the dinar
through greater business efficiency in general,

      To assure a much faster growth of exports over
production and a slightly slower increase of imports
relative to exports, accompanied by a rational and
profitable regional distribution of exports and
imports,

      To build up substantial foreign exchange re-
serves,

      To adjust the level of external indebtedness and
of export-financing credits to the country's balance-of-
payments potentialities. [6]

In attempting to achieve these goals, a number of steps were
taken which cannot be regarded as a new development but rather an
acceleration of the process that began in 1952. The reforms were
comprehensive, including all the component systems of the foreign
trade system. The component systems present a convenient vehicle
for discussing the reforms and will be used for this purpose. However,
we will begin with an important aspect of the Economic Reform that
is not classified in this manner.

A basic element of the Economic Reform was the overhaul of
the price system. By the early months of 1965, price controls covered
between 70 and 80 percent of industrial production. The establishment
of scarcity prices was of evident importance to the foreign trade
system. Scarcity prices would permit a rational determination of

which products to export or import. An example of one such price
reform was a more uniform application of the turnover tax so that
it would not distort relative prices to such a large degree.

> The first step was to clear the state, and this is what
> has now been largely done. The arrangements for
> foreign trade have been greatly simplified and the
> turnover tax has also been made more uniform. It
> would not be surprising, however, if in due course,
> differences in the rate of tax on different commodities
> were to be widened a little. This would not mean
> that the current phase of greater uniformity was a
> mistake. On the contrary, whatever may be
> attempted later, the old jungle had first to be cleared. [7]

Such price reforms are by no means complete at present. There
has been some backsliding and many distortions remain. Of these
distortions, the low payment for some uses of capital and frozen
price (in some markets) cause the greatest problems in the foreign
trade sector. The price reform did, however, have effects.

> The immediate effect was an average increase in
> prices of 24 percent; the prices of agricultural
> products, transportation, construction, and various
> services increased by 32, 26, 22, and 45, respec-
> tively, and industrial goods, on the average, by 14
> percent. [8]

The first of the three components of the foreign trade system,
the export-import system, has experienced a reform of degree.
This system consists primarily of the regulations regarding trading
enterprises and traded goods. The reform in this system has primarily consisted of the relaxation of restrictions on obtaining licenses
to engage in foreign trade and a drop in the number of items on restricted import lists.

> The exportation of all those articles which are not
> covered by the special list of licensed exports is free.
> In other words, the exporters themselves decide
> what, how much, and where they will export. The
> program of exports which is established every year
> by the administrative authority within the framework
> of the Federal Social Plan only serves to orientate
> the enterprises.
>   "Free exports" means that exporters may export

the products which are not covered by the list of products subject to licensing without any trade restrictions.
However, all exporters are bound to sell the foreign
exchange deriving to them from exports to the National
Bank regardless of whether freely exportable or other
goods are involved. Thus, freedom from trade restrictions does not imply freedom from exchange restrictions, too, considering that the said compulsory
surrender of foreign exchange to the bank constitutes
a typical measure of exchange control. Furthermore,
free export does not imply that everyone is free to
export. . . . As for the country's import trade, the
following categories are distinguished: free imports,
conditionally free imports, imports subject to quota,
imports on the basis of the global exchange quota, and
imports on the basis of license.[9]

These restricted import lists have generally been relaxed as a result
of the Economic Reform. (Most of the products for personal consumption are covered by lists subject to quota.) However, there has
been backsliding on this issue also. From 1967 to 1968, the number
of items covered by the restricted list almost quadrupled (from 5
percent of listed import numbers in 1967 to 19 per cent in 1968).[10]

In addition to the export-import-license relaxation, there has
also been a change in the law concerning foreign investment in Yugoslavia. In mid-1967, some foreign investment was allowed. (The
demise of this Communist taboo was the subject of such discussion
by the East European participants in the 1970 Summer Seminar in
Grado, Italy, sponsored by the Thomas Jefferson Center, University
of Virginia, and CESES, Milan, Italy. The Polish and Hungarian
participants expressed strong opposition to this "new course" the
Yugoslavs had taken.)[11]

The tariff system reform has been aimed at the reduction of
tariff barriers.* In an early plan, enterprises were warned that
tariffs and subsidies would only be granted industries that could
prove that they could shortly become competitive.

Under 1961 reforms, only temporary protection in the
form of customs tariffs and subsidies will be given

---

*Export and import tariffs and quotas are included in this
reform.

industries seeking protection, and such recipients
must first demonstrate that they can quickly meet
foreign competition. [12]

The plan justified tariffs only in the case of infant industries and put
the proof of such infancy on the industry. This "threat" was never
carried through. However, Yugoslav planners have greatly reduced
tariffs. Branislav Soskic reported at the CESES Sorrento Seminar
that:

. . . domestic production is less protected. Even
though customs tariffs for certain products are still
pretty high (more than 30 per cent), the average
customs tariffs have been decreased from over 20
percent to about 11 percent, so that these customs
tariffs are lower than in all other countries. [13]

Yugoslavia seems not to be caught up in the always popular game of
demanding reciprocal tariff reductions. There seems to be realization
of the gains to be made even if such tariff reductions are not recipro-
cated. These tariff cuts are described in greater detail by the United
Nations.

The new tariff is a one-column tariff, but with a 50
percent increase in rates for countries which do not
extend to Yugoslavia most-favored-nation treatment.
It is based on the Brussels Tariff Nomenclature and
the Convention of Values. The average tariff in-
cidence has been reduced from 23.3 percent to 11.7
percent; for raw materials from 12.14 to 5.11 percent; for semi-manufactured products from 17.9 to
9.26 percent; for capital goods from 42.79 to 20.39
percent; and for consumers' goods from 43.16 to
21.06 percent. Imports of tropical foodstuffs are
now duty-free. [14]

The tariff reform has also experienced the partial retreat we have
witnessed earlier. The Customs Tariff Act (1965) set the final stage
for this reform and GATT admission. The Yugoslav Government
has since increased tariffs in response to balance of payments pressures caused by increased imports.* "In May, 1968, legislation was

---

*For figures on this import surge, see Chapter 3.

adopted introducing a special levy on imported goods as a means of
adjustment to charges levied on domestic products. . . ."[15] This
new tariff system is unique among the countries in Eastern Europe
in that it closely conforms to that of Western countries. The nomenclature follows the Brussels Customs Nomenclature and the law has
provisions very similar to those found in Western countries. This
was done to conform to the GATT framework and to participate in
the Kennedy Round.[16]

The reform of the third component system, the foreign exchange
system, has progressed most slowly. This has been the lagging
sector in the complete reform of foreign trade, which will proceed
only as fast as progress in the slowest sector. The distortions caused
by multiple exchange rates will work to negate the reform of prices
and tariffs. Likewise, the reform of the export-import sector, allowing
all firms to engage in trade in response to market forces, has little
effect if these firms are denied control over their exchange earnings.

Reform of the foreign exchange sector was attempted in an
effort to correct these problems. In the summer of 1952 the dinar
was devalued from 50 dinars per $1 (U.S.) to 300 dinars per $1. All
foreign exchange earnings were paid to the Central Bank and multiple
exchange rates were in effect.[17] In 1961, the exchange rate was
further reduced to 1/750 of $1. The 1965 Economic Reform again
devalued the dinar and did away with the multiple rates. Prior to
1965, the average export exchange rate per $1 by sector of the economy
was as follows:

Industry and mining	1114 dinars
Agriculture	918 dinars
Forestry	860 dinars
Transport	1001 dinars
Tourism*	915 dinars[18]

The Economic Reform set the exchange rate for all sectors at 1250
dinars per $1.** On the official record this appears as a large
devaluation, but is "really for about 15 percent with regard to the

---

*This rate was favorable to exporters of finished goods and
penalized traditional sectors.

**A new dinar was defined to be at a rate of 12.5 new dinars
per $1.

average export rate of exchange, and by about 25 percent with regards
to the average import rate of exchange."[19] A further devaluation
occurred on January 23, 1971. This devaluation set a new par value
of 15 new dinars per $1.

The devaluation of the dinar, a step necessary to achieve the
introduction of foreign exchange markets and the dinar's convertibility,
has not achieved this goal. Foreign exchange markets and convertibility are probably quite far in the future. At present, as a conse-
quence of the 1965 Economic Reform, exporters are allowed control
of only 7 percent of their foreign exchange earnings.

The reforms discussed above are bold in intent. Many of the
consequences are already being felt by the Yugoslav economy. The
reforms must be viewed in the proper context. Restrictions on trade
and exchange have by no means been abolished. Imports are, in
general, still restricted by the rationing process used in foreign
exchange dealings. Additionally, the 1965 devaluation did not give
the anticipated advantage to Yugoslav goods.* B. Horvat has gone
so far as to say, "None of the objectives quoted by Anakioski was
achieved."[20] Apart from the problems that remain, the real significance of the reform is the conscious effort to strengthen the positive
impact of foreign criteria on the Yugoslav economy.

Western appraisals of the Yugoslav reforms are generally
optimistic concerning future progress. Such progress, in the light
of East European hostility, seems closely linked with Yugoslavia's
ability to remain independent. Any exogenous shock (perhaps even
the death of Tito) could cause political disruption leading to a re-
petition of the Czechoslovakian August. All this underscores the
ideological schism in Eastern Europe. Experiences in the Soviet
Union, East Germany, and Poland indicate a renewal of restriction
on reforms and reformers. Stefan Stolte, in a recent review of
Comecon, reported on the conflict centering on such reform movements:

> Thus the "essence of socialist democracy" is for
> Ulbricht "a higher standard of organization and
> discipline" subject to the absolute direction of the
> Party Leaders. . . ; Ulbricht replies to the
> Yugoslav and Czechoslovak reformers: "Socialist

---

*The Yugoslav inflation obliterated any effect of the 1965 de-
valuation on foreign trade.

democracy has nothing in common with bourgeois
'self-management, ' even if it is called socialist. "
From the very beginning, the conservative Communists have wanted to modernize the economy by
means of technology and science rather than by
social and political reform. Thus, conservative
Communism not only denies the workers all right
to self-management through the election of officers
and control of their work, but allows the managers
themselves little independence and room for initiative. It still insists upon centralized planning,
and absolutely rejects the possibility of regarding
the market and free or partly free prices as a
regulating factor, as they are regarded even today
in Yugoslavia and Hungary. Thus, Antonin Kapek, a
post-intervention member (and presidium member)
of the Czechoslovak Party Central Committee, and
the Soviet economist Lev Leontev (Leontyev) wrote
in a joint study: "Of late, imperialist theorists
have been trying to palm off on the socialist countries the concept of a 'market socialism, ' denoting
rejection of planned management and a free play of
the spontaneous market forces. " Such admonitions,
really directed at Communists such as Tito and
Dubcek, and not against the "imperialists, " cannot
hide the fact that although the forces of serious
economic reform are, to a greater or lesser degree,
still at work in most of the Comecon countries, they
are being increasingly threatened by a kind of re-
Stalinization.[21]

The reform movement in Yugoslavia is by far the most ambitious
and thorough of any in Eastern Europe. Success (or failure) may
well indicate the future of such reforms for all the bloc countries. If
a stable, new system does emerge, the experience may be attractive
to the other bloc countries.

THE REFORM AND STATE TRADING

The economic reform movements discussed in the preceding
section have all helped to increase the autonomy of the enterprise.

Since the introduction of self-management in the
country's economy the evolution of the Yugoslav

system of foreign trade has been distinguished by an
increasing freedom of enterprises in the matter of
decision-making and initiative in international economic relations. When the system of State monopoly
in foreign trade was definitely abandoned in 1952,
there followed a period characterized by the establishment of more liberal relationships in the sphere of
the economy as well. [22]

As we have discussed this process of "sensitizing" the economy of
world markets, we have been talking about Western markets. However,
the Comecon countries do account for a substantial share of Yugoslavia's foreign trade. The reform literature says little about this
trade. T. Wilson and G. R. Denton do report that

So far as the pattern of trading relations is concerned,
the aim is to achieve a balanced structure such that
some 35-40 percent of trade is with Comecon countries, 40 percent with Western industrial countries
and 7-8 percent with developing nations. Comecon trade
is centrally planned on the ground that Yugoslavia has to
deal with the State trading organizations in Comecon
countries. But trade with Western countries, and with
the "third world", is expected to be the outcome of
trading arrangements freely entered into by autonomous
Yugoslav enterprises. From 1 January 1967, any
enterprise has had complete freedom to sell either on
the home or on the foreign markets. [23]

This exception to the liberal reform movement, the adherence
to state trading for dealing with the Comecon countries, is motivated
by the bilateral nature of this trade. Yugoslavia must operate from
the same infrastructure in order to countervail the powerful state
organizations in Comecon.*

----

*A private discussion with Professor L. Adamovich, University
of Belgrade, made this problem with Comecon trade more clear.
He felt that dealing with the monopolies presented a problem to the
Yugoslavs. They were unsure of how it should be carried out; they
did, however, recognize the importance of maintaining the state
monopoly. He saw danger in allowing enterprises to maximize their
own position, arguing that they would compete, through prices, for
exports to the USSR.

FIGURE 1

Agreements on Clearing

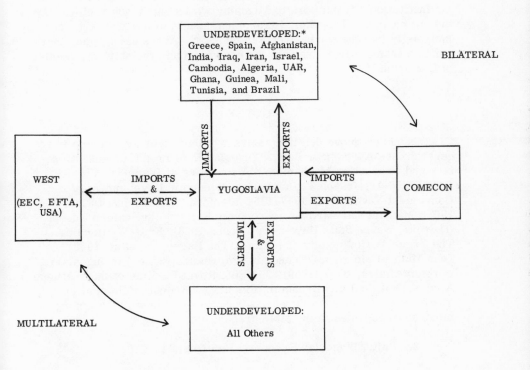

Source: Yugoslav Foreign Trade Almanac (Belgrade: 1968), p. 95.

Yugoslavia maintains bilateral economic relations with 25 countries (see Figure 1). The largest percentage of this trade is carried out with the countries of Comecon. The Federal Secretary of Foreign Trade on the Federal Executive Council prescribes the way in which this trade is to be carried out. Much of this trade is barter trade and is under the direct control of the Federal Executive Council. In addition to being bilateral, many of the trade agreements cover long periods of time.* This evidence presents a dichotomy in the institutional framework of Yugoslavia's foreign trade sector. On the one hand, the Economic Reform has sought to integrate the economy more fully into the world (Western) market. At the same time, there exists a framework to insulate the economy from the state monopolies of Comecon.**

NOTES

1. For a more detailed analysis of the Yugoslav reforms in general, see Aleksander Bajt, "Yugoslav Economic Reforms, Monetary and Production Mechanism," Economics of Planning, VII, 3 (1967), 200-18; Joseph T. Bombelles, Economic Development of Communist Yugoslavia, 1947-1964 (Stanford: Hoover Institution, 1968); Michael Garmarnikov, Economic Reforms in Eastern Europe (Detroit: Wayne State University Press, 1968); Frits W. Hondius, The Yugoslav Community of Nations (The Hague: Mouton, 1968); John Michael Montias, "Economic Reform and Retreat in Jugoslavia," Foreign Affairs, 37-2 (1959), 291-305; Royal Institute of International Affairs, Political and Economic Planning, "Economic Reform in Yugoslavia" (Greenwich Research Publications, July 1968); among other sources listed in the bibliography.

2. Bajt, "Yugoslav Economic Reforms," p. 200.

3. Garmarnikov, Economic Reforms in Eastern Europe, p. 72.

4. Bicanic, "Economics of Socialism in a Developed Country," Foreign Affairs, XLIV, 4 (1966), 634.

---

*Appendix B summarizes the instruments regulating commodity trade between Yugoslavia and the Comecon countries.

**The implication of this dichotomy will be the subject of the remainder of this study.

5. Hondius, Yugoslav Community, p. 320.

6. Dusan Anakioski, "Foreign Trade in the Years of the Reform," Yugoslav Survey, X, 3 (August 1969), 71.

7. T. Wilson and G. R. Denton, "Plans and Markets in Yugoslavia," Economic Reform in Yugoslavia, PEP (July 1968), p. 233.

8. Secretariat of the Economic Commission for Europe, The European Economy in 1965, United Nations, p. 64.

9. Institute of Comparative Law, The Foreign Trade, Foreign Exchange, and Customs Systems (Belgrade: Federation of Jurists Association, 1968), pp. 4-5.

10. Milorod Savicevic, "Protective Tariffs and Other Measures of Protection of the National Economy," Yugoslav Survey, XI (February 1970), p. 58.

11. See Hondius, Yugoslav Community of Nations, and M. Sukijasovic, Yugoslav Foreign Investment Legislation at Work: Experiences so Far (Dobbs Ferry, N.Y.: Oceana Publications, 1970).

12. George Macesich, Yugoslavia: The Theory and Practice of Development Planning (Charlottesville: The University Press of Virginia, 1964), p. 194.

13. Thomas Jefferson Center, University of Virginia and CESES, Milan, Italy, "Current Problems of Economic Planning in Eastern Europe," Sorrento Seminar, July 1968, p. 38 (mimeographed).

14. Secretariat of the Economic Commission for Europe, European Economy, p. 48.

15. Savicevic, "Protective Tariffs," p. 57.

16. See Institute of Comparative Law, Foreign Trade, for a listing of this law.

17. Bombelles, Development of Communist Yugoslavia, p. 100.

18. Ibid., p. 63.

19. Saviceric, "Protective Tariffs," p. 56.

20. Horvat, "Yugoslav Economic Policy in the Post-War Period: Problems, Ideas, Institutional Developments," American Economic Review, LXI, 3 (June 1971), 127.

21. Stefan C. Stolte, "Comecon on the Threshold of the Seventies," Bulletin, Institute for the Study of the USSR, XVII (July 1970), pp. 20-21.

22. Institute of Comparative Law, Foreign Trade, p. 3.

23. T. Wilson and G. R. Denton, "Plans and Markets in Yugoslavia," p. 230.

5

THE EFFECTS
OF STATE TRADING

The literature on the effects of state trading is extensive. From their inception state trading monopolies were thought to be discriminatory. This chapter will examine the literature concerning the discrimination effects of state trading.

STATE TRADING AND DISCRIMINATION:
A SURVEY OF RECENT LITERATURE

Lacking better criteria, this survey will follow, as closely as possible, the chronological order of the literature. The studies that attempt empirical verification will be presented after those that are primarily descriptive in nature.

Discussion of the effects of state trading in the socialist bloc began in the early 1940s. Jacob Viner argued that these state trading monopolies must, by the very nature of their existence, exercise their inherent power.[1]

When monopoly power is present, its use tends, to some
extent, to be automatic and undeliberate. The existence
of the power, even without conscious will to exploit it,
is sufficient to yield some monopolistic fruits.[2]

Viner also recognized that the existence of one state trading monopoly would mean that other state trading monopolies would come into exist-ence. He argued that because the trading practices within the bloc would be on the basis of bilateral monopoly, to protect itself from injury, a country would be forced to make an ad hoc agreement with the state trading country. This meant that monopoly was being met by monopoly. Viner recognized that the self-righteous claims of the Soviet Union that all socialist countries would share equally in the "socialist commonwealth of nations" were purely political rhetoric. At an early date, he pointed out that attempts at bloc autarky would suffer at the expense of national autarky, recognizing that these state monopolies would automatically interfere with trade. He felt the question was only how much and what kind of interference. "Private enterprise, as such, is normally unpatriotic, while government is automatically patriotic. "[3]

Wassily Leontief, in discussing aspects of labor union wage negotiations, drew an analogy to the state monopolies as approaching the perfectly discriminating monopolist who combines price fixing with quantity fixing. [4] Leontief argued that the labor union that bargained both the wage rate and the work week was analogous to the state monopoly that bargained price and quantity.

In the late 1940s and early 1950s, economists were becoming increasingly interested in the monopoly effects of these state monopolies. These interests were fed by accusations of wrongdoing filtering out of Eastern Europe. Typical is a Yugoslav complaint reported in the New York Times. [5] The Yugoslavs denounced the Russians for buying Rumanian oil at world prices, which were below Rumanian costs, and selling it to Hungary and Czechoslovakia at Soviet domestic prices, which were considerably above world market prices.* Such reports increased Western interest in the Soviet monopoly and her captive trading partners.

Edward Ames, primarily as a result of such reports, attempted to determine how a "fair" price is determined in intrabloc trade. [6] He quoted Voprosy Ekonomiki that all prices and quantities are fixed by trade agreements and that each exporting country charges the same price to all bloc countries.

Spulber and Gehrels, reacting to these same reports, argued that

Despite the provisions to use world prices, it might be inferred from some indirect evidence, that price

─────────────

*World prices being the standard to ensure "fair" treatment to all bloc nations.

discrimination, in favor of the Soviet Union, existed especially in the earlier years. Data on export unit values
for Czechoslovakia for 1948 suggests that her exports to
the Soviet Union might have been sold at lower prices
than her exports to the other East European countries.
In addition, according to Yugoslav sources, the Soviet
Union has resold on world markets goods imported from
Eastern Europe, presumably at a profit. Such abuses
and the Yugoslav attacks may be responsible for a joint
decision of these countries, publicized in their press,
from 1951 on, against price discrimination within the
orbit. Prices in the trade agreements are determined
by the relative bargaining strengths of the trading partners. *[7]

John Hazard, writing at this time, reported that these suspicions of the wrongdoing by the Soviet trading monopoly had per-
meated American foreign policy. [8] Similarly, James Reston, writing
in the December 2, 1958, <u>New York Times</u> reported that

We have been discussing quietly inside our Government for six months the need to establish an overseas
trade monopoly to compete with the Soviet monopoly
on equal terms. [9]

Don Humphrey, in 1959, attempted to specify the determinants
of the bargaining strength of a state trading monopoly. [10] He argued
that the effects of state trading can be viewed as a tax on imports
and exports, having similar results.** Humphrey pointed out that the
bargaining position of a state monopoly is dependent on the elasticity
of demand for its exports and its elasticity of demand for imports.
Additionally, the elasticity of the export supply of the rest of the
world may be counted as a determinant of the importing country's

---

*It is impossible for the same price to be charged to all mem-
bers and these prices to be determined by the relative strengths of
the partners.

**It should be noted, however, that while the state trading
automatically limits the flow of trade to the quantity agreed upon,
a tax interferes with the trade but does not limit the amount. State
trading is, therefore, analogous to a system of quotas.

bargaining position. * Another determinant of the bargaining position
is the cost of shifting resources from export producing to import
competing production. If this cost is low, the bargaining position of
the state trading monopoly is increased.

An article appearing in the same issue of Law and Contemporary Problems discussed the problems that state trading presented
to international organizations. J. E. S. Fawcett was concerned with
the notion that state trading with its bilateral negotiations is contrary
to the most-favored-nation clause. [11] He argued that the most-favored-
nation clause incorporated in the institutional framework of state
trading can only mean freedom of opportunity to negotiate.

In still another article in this same issue devoted to state
trading, Nicolas Spulber concentrated on the formation of intrabloc
prices. [12] He described the trade negotiations as being carried out
by the "operational" section of the ministry of foreign trade. These
negotiations result in a draft; "The draft specifies the volume, prices,
and transport costs, structure and direction of foreign trade. "[13]
These prices, Spulber argued, "take into account" the prices prevailing on world markets. These prices are then left unchanged
for at least one year and usually longer.

In his book published in 1960, Robert Allen pictured state
trading as the transformation of economic decisions into economic-
political-military decisions. [14]

Allen argued that state trading results in price discrimination,
among a multitude of other sins.

> . . . with control over a part or all of its trade, a nation
> may use this trade to reward its friends, punish its
> enemies, to extract economic and political concessions,
> and to influence decisions not only of trading partners
> but also of third countries. [15]

Frederic L. Pryor's work, done in East Germany, does much
to illuminate the operation of the state trading monopoly in intrabloc

---

*In the same manner, the elasticity of demand for imports
of third countries will affect the bargaining position.

dealings.[16]* Of primary interest are the criteria used to determine prices in intrabloc trade. The dialogue has changed rapidly, and at times, it is impossible to determine what the bases for such prices are. (Pryor reports that four different criteria have been used for determining prices. From 1946-50, world prices, at the time of the signing of the contract, were used. From 1951-53, the "era of stop-prices" existed. Because of the price increases of the Korean boom, 1950 prices were used. In the 1954-57 period, "the so-called adjusted prices were used." These were adjusted stop-prices. Since 1958, Pryor feels the basis of prices is difficult to determine, probably because a combination of criteria are applied.)[17]

In recent years, prices are quite probably determined through bargaining, which uses the average price on free markets as a be- ginning point. Pryor reported that, quite apart from the political diatribes about proletarian equality, "from a description of the way in which prices are negotiated, it seems quite likely that they are set in very heated bargaining sessions."[18] These sessions, as the following incidents highlight, are indicative of what one might expect in negotiations between bilateral monopolies. Pryor related the testimony of a Bulgarian foreign trade adviser during Russian pro- ceedings.

> The Soviet Union had a certain interest in our tobacco.
> Since we knew about this, we decided to offer a smaller
> amount (than expected) and in this way, to cause diffi-
> culties in the negotiations. . . .[19]

In a similar example, Wiles describes the show trials of the ranking communist leaders of Bulgaria and Czechoslovakia; Kostov and Slansky, respectively. These leaders were accused by Stalin of Titoism. Both leaders admitted to "unfair" trading practices against the Soviet Union. "Prices above the 'world' level were asked for exports and prices below it offered for imports. Commercial secrecy was maintained vis-à-vis Soviet negotiators. (!) The quantity of exports was kept low in order to prolong negotiations."[20] Wiles mentions that this "offering" of small quantities did not affect prices

---

*Pryor was arrested while conducting interviews in East Germany. For five and one-half months he was held incommunicado and was interrogated almost daily by the East German Secret Police. His book represents what was reportedly the evidence of his "spy- ing."

because they were bargained separately. If the bargaining position
was strengthened by offering low quantities, it would automatically
have an effect on the price negotiating sessions. Further incidents
are even more illuminating. In 1951, an assistant foreign trade
minister of Czechoslovakia wrote:

> The foreign trade enterprises, according to my instruc-
> tions, asked the USSR for prices quite high above the
> prices of the world market. They demanded, with my
> approval and according to my instructions, prices 30%
> higher than those which we received from the capitalist
> countries for our exports of crankshafts, generators,
> electric motors, and oil pipes. [21]

Another Czechoslovak assistant minister stated in 1952 that

> I know that this parasitical work [offering goods only
> at extra high prices] is more observable in those sec-
> tors of machinery building which are the most important
> link between Czechoslovakia and the other countries of
> the democratic [CMEA] camp. [22]*

Pryor goes on to describe the tactics used in these bargaining sessions.
He pointed out that market information was scarce and, as a result,
was a source of power. The Soviet monopoly used this knowledge
gap to its advantage. Fritz Schenis, a top East German defector,
related to Pryor the method the Russians used in gathering information.

> The Soviets had knowledge of every important price agree-
> ment which the DDR [German Democratic Republic] made
> with other bloc nations since the results of these negotia-
> tions were written up on Russian-German form sheets with
> one copy going to the DDR Ministry of Foreign Trade and
> another to the Russian Embassy. This practice lasted
> through 1956, and may still be in use.[23]

The value placed on this information by the Russians may help to
explain Pryor's arrest in East Germany for "spying. "

----

*These two quotations point out the obvious; the monopoly
power was strongest where demand was more inelastic.

The use of tie-in sales is another manifestation of this monopoly power. The result of his interviews in Eastern Europe led Pryor to conclude that ". . . negotiation sessions between the Bloc nations have not always been ruled by the harmony doctrine of proletarian internationalism."[24]

Sidney Dell, in discussing East-West trading in light of the foreign trade monopolies, argued that these monopolies present no obstacles to trade.[25] He believed that the "lumpiness" of East European dealings puts them at a disadvantage in negotiations, despite the fact that trading takes place through the monopoly. Dell felt that the main deterrent to increased East-West trade is the desire for autarky, or more specifically, the fear that trade will be stopped if the country becomes dependent on such trade.*

G. Haberler has noted the dichotomy existing between the theory of socialist planning and what experience indicates to be the case.[26] In an article, Haberler drew attention to the lack of trade theory in socialist literature. Oscar Lange, in his famous "On the Economic Theory of Socialism," does not even mention international trade.[27] H. D. Dickinson mentioned trade relations with noncommunist countries only briefly.[28] He referred to intrabloc trade in a single footnote, in which he said that there is no need to worry about intrasocialist trade because socialism is free of nationalistic bias. He does not share the Marxian belief that the state will wither, but "all that would be necessary is to instruct the managers of plants and industries in each country to disregard national boundaries and to refrain from 'discrimination.'"[29] Haberler argued that this naive view is ludicrous. Nationalism has not died—rather, it has grown more powerful in recent years. He pointed out that planners in Soviet countries are probably more patriotic than their counterparts in Western countries.**

G. Warren Nutter has argued that the increasing trend in the bloc countries to trade with the West is a deliberate effort to introduce competition into their economy.[30] He added,

---

*This is also a relevant point in intrabloc trade. Yugoslavia has experienced such a blockade, but it was at the hand of the Soviets, rather than Western nations.

**One is reminded of the way Viner phrases it, as quoted above, "Private enterprise, as such, is normally nonpatriotic, while government is automatically patriotic."

Economists of Eastern Europe are also well aware of
the need for open trading to extend their markets and
develop gains from specialization. To accomplish this
end, these countries must first alter the closed trading
system of the Soviet bloc, whose primary purpose has
been to facilitate exploitation by the Soviet Union.[31]

In the final article we will mention before turning to the empirical investigations, Jan Michal re-emphasized the lack of a rational
pricing criteria in intrabloc trade.[32] He argued that the Comecon
trade has been conducted at world market prices, with the same
world market standard existing for a long period of time.

This survey of recent literature attests to the wide variety
of opinions on the effects of state trading. Viner and Haberler hold
the typical Western belief that these monopolies cannot help but
exercise their discriminatory power. This notion is at odds with
Eastern political statements embracing the "harmony doctrine of
proletarian internationalism" that exists within the "socialist commonwealth of nations. " Beyond general agreement on the point of discrimination, the Western economists tend to diverge in their other
opinions. The articles by Pryor, Michal, and Spulber accent the
problem of price determination. They conclude that prices quite
probably are based on "free-world" market prices, but the evidence
indicates heated bargaining, which one would expect between state
monopolies. Nutter and Allen are in agreement that a primary result
of state trading is price discrimination.

Publication of trade statistics by some East European countries
has stimulated empirical investigation into the effects of these state-
trading monopolies. We will now, briefly, examine this recent
empirical literature.

The first of the empirical studies dealing with the question of
discrimination in the intrabloc trading relations is the work done
by Horst Mendershausen. Mendershausen statistically demonstrated
that the Soviet Union, using its monopolistic-monopsonistic power,
was able to discriminate against her East European trading partners.[33]
His work, which will be briefly sketched, showed consistent price
differentials when he compared Soviet terms of trade with the West,
against the terms of trade with the bloc countries.

Mendershausen used Soviet data to obtain his terms of trade
figures. Since prices were not available, he calculated "average

unit values. "* These values were calculated for 47 to 64 percent of
Soviet exports to the satellites, and 57 to 71 percent of Soviet exports to noncommunist Europe during the period 1955-59. On the
import side, the data were not as comprehensive. The sample consisted of from 18 to 24 import items that represented 4 to 6 percent
of imports from the satellites and from 10 to 13 percent of Soviet
imports from West Europe. [34] The sample of import items was, in
part, restricted because of the large number of items the Soviet Union
imported only from noncommunist Europe. The calculated "average
unit values" were interpreted as reflecting prices at the Soviet fron-
tier. Therefore, different "average unit values" for the same commodity groups indicated different prices. "Qualitative differences
in the composition of the commodity categories from country to
country were assumed to be unsystematic with regard to the political
color of the country. "[35] Likewise, for transport costs, there was
no evidence that the costs were higher (or lower) for exports to
either group. "It is our guess that better information on qualities
and shipping costs than is now available would weaken the tendencies
established by this study in some instances, and strengthen them in
others. "[36]

Mendershausen's first study covered the years 1955-57 and
discovered that the "average unit values, " i.e., the price of Soviet
exports to the satellites, exceeded the price of exports to West
Europe for a majority of the commodities. The later study for
1958-59 showed the same pattern, but with far fewer exceptions.

In 1958, Soviet exports to the Satellites showed higher
average unit values than to Free Europe for 41 out of
49 commodities (compared with 32 out of 48 in 1957);
and the ratios of Satellite to Free Europe unit values
increased (i.e., became less favorable to the Satellites)
for 32 of these Soviet export commodities. This tendency
continued in 1959; 29 of 46 positions showed less favorable
unit values for the Satellites than in 1958. [37]

---

*This is done by dividing the number of units (or other measure
of quantity) imported or exported into the money value of the bundle
of exports or imports. Since unit quantities for all commodities
were not available, "average unit values" could not be calculated
for all cases.

Mendershausen argued that this phenomenon was partly the result of
the way in which prices are determined for intrabloc trade. The
prices for next year's trade are set on this year's price experience.
In other words, the prices do not reflect the prices at which self-
regulating markets will be cleared next year.

> The "world market price standard" used in Bloc trade
> is, therefore, likely to show a systematic lag behind
> actual price movements in the market economies, to
> underprice exports in the Bloc when world prices go up,
> and to overprice them when world prices go down. This
> tendency seems to have been at work throughout this
> period, accounting for some lessening of Soviet export
> price discrimination against the Satellites between 1955
> and 1957 and a fresh increase of discrimination from
> 1957 to 1958 and 1959. [38]

The study showed substantial discrimination against the satellite
countries. Additionally, study of particular export commodities
furnished interesting details on trade by country. The prices paid
by the satellite countries were not similar. This individual discrimination is the result of the bilateral nature of Soviet trade. These
different prices persist, despite the supposedly common price standard. This contradicts the following quotation cited by Mendershausen
from a Soviet text on political economy.

> Commodity prices on the world market of the socialist
> Bloc countries are stable. They are fixed through vol-
> untary agreement between partners enjoying equal rights,
> with mutual interests fully observed. This excludes any
> kind of discrimination or non-equivalence in exchange.
> The multiplicity of prices characteristic of the foreign
> trade of capitalistic countries is absent. [39]

Mendershausen calculated an "average price" charged the bloc countries and found that,

> Bulgaria, Albania, Hungary, and Rumania did worse
> by this standard than did the seven Satellites as a group;
> Poland and Czechoslovakia did better. East Germany
> suffered a degree of price discrimination equal to the
> average for all. The three Westernmost Satellites fared
> best. [40]

This might indicate that the bargaining position of the Soviet Union
was tempered by the greater ease of substituting Western goods.

Mendershausen's investigation of the import side is undermined by the smallness of his sample. From his sample he concluded that the Soviet Union was also able to discriminate on imports. He again discovered the slow adjustment to world prices much as it appeared in the export sector.

In his conclusion, Mendershausen calculated that the total price discrimination (over the five-year period), as measured by the samples, amounted to 70 percent of the reported cumulative Soviet export surplus.* That is likely to be an underestimate if the sample can be regarded as reflecting the total export and import movement.

In summarizing the work done by Mendershausen, we reviewed his argument, which claimed that the Soviet Union has effectively practiced price discrimination against the smaller bloc countries. This discrimination varied over time and between countries.

The second study on the question of Soviet discrimination takes exception to the view of Mendershausen.[41] Franklyn D. Holzman felt Mendershausen erred in his failure to look upon the "Soviet bloc of nations as a type of customs union. " He argued that this "customs union" operates in such a way to conduct a maximum amount of trade within the bloc, going outside only when necessary.** The cost of this autarkic policy is often reflected in the satellite countries' selling exports below and buying imports above the West Europe price. Holzman argued that this Soviet discrimination was often in favor of the bloc, and sometimes against the bloc. A different calculation of what was a "fair" price must be made, but not on the basis of a comparison of West Europe and bloc terms of trade. Holzman argued that Mendershausen did not measure discrimination but, rather, losses to the bloc nations, of restricting their trade to the Soviet Union.

Critics have contended that if this "customs union" is held together by Soviet political power, this "cost" of union autarky is, in effect, discrimination. Pryor quotes an East German economist referring to the use of such force. "No country should be forced to buy an item for more than what it can pay for it in another country. "[42]

---

*Mendershausen is demonstrating that 70 percent of USSR "aid" in this period was a "return" on the amount of price discrimination.

**This contention could easily be tested by examining the composition of imports and exports into and out of the bloc nations.

Holzman's argument that the measured price differentials represent
bloc losses incurred by restricting trade might be viewed as gains
to the Soviet Union caused by "holding" the bloc nations captive.

Holzman devised another method of measuring bloc discrimination. He examined intrabloc prices per se. If different prices
were charged different countries, then there was evidence of discrimination. His evidence indicated that the bloc countries and the
Soviet Union discriminated in their intrabloc trading relations. A
closer look will be given to Holzman's most recent contribution. [43]

In the article, Holzman claimed to refute the discrimination
argument (based on comparisons with Western Europe). He showed
that Bulgaria discriminated against the Soviet Union and the rest
of the bloc to a greater degree than did the Soviet Union. He concluded that since Bulgaria did not have the type of bargaining power
that Mendershausen credits Russia with, the use of this measure
is wrong for the purpose of measuring discrimination.

> To sum up: with the exception of Polish imports, Bul-
> garian and Polish "discrimination" patterns are even
> more pronounced than those found by Mendershausen
> for the USSR. This would seem to refute the usefulness
> of comparisons with Western Europe to prove "discrim-
> ination." [44]

Secondly, he measured "Western discrimination against the
bloc." "That is to say, to the extent that bloc nations are forced
to export at lower prices to Western Europe than to Eastern Europe,
one should find West European nations importing from each other
at higher prices than from Eastern Europe." [45] Holzman then measured
the use of Soviet bargaining power against the bloc. He examined
intrabloc trade per se, "because it eliminates the extraneous factors
of (1) Western discrimination, and (2) the differences in price patterns
between the fairly insulated markets of East and West." [46] His figures
show the Soviets were able to discriminate against the bloc. The
discrimination is measured as deviations from prices in intrabloc
trade.

These first two empirical investigations deserve further comparison. Indeed, the interchange was carried out in subsequent
notes. [47] Mendershausen believed that Holzman's results are not
all inconsistent with his findings: "They add to them and generalize
them." [48] He argued that the discrimination system appears to be
multilateral and mutual.

> The monopolistic-monopsonistic position that I attributed
> to the USSR in much of her trade with the Satellites is
> accompanied by certain monopolistic positions of various
> bloc countries vis-à-vis the others. [49]

He argued that this monopolistic element inherent in the system
is often strengthened by production planning. He cited the assign-
ment of the production of heavy trucks to Rumania, medium trucks
to Hungary, and light trucks to East Germany.* Holzman seemed to
overlook the fact that, besides bloc autarky, each country tends to
strive for national autarky. In his final defense, Mendershausen
attributed a clear role to the Soviet Union. It created and maintained
captive partners in a fenced-in area.

There appears to be more controversy than there need be.
Holzman shows intrabloc discrimination, using intrabloc data per se.**
This measure of discrimination shows a type of countervailing bargaining between the monopoly trading sectors. Mendershausen con-
curs with this demonstration. However, he correctly wants to compare
the action of these monopolies to free-world markets. He argues:

> . . . There remains a great interest in relating this
> behavior to the operations of these monopolies in the
> free-world markets; for this permits us to test the
> assertions of non-discriminating market behavior
> across the board, which are being made on behalf of
> the monopolies. The testing is of interest as long as
> critics inside and outside the Bloc question the relations
> between prices and costs of the trade monopolies and
> between their prices at one "counter" and at another,
> and are not satisfied with the sanctimonious declamations
> about their price policies. [50]

The two authors, though not in complete agreement, have drawn
attention to effects of the state trading monopolies.

---

*These assignments are often ignored because of the desire
for (or fear of) national policies toward autarky.

**Holzman correctly points out that it is impossible for all
to discriminate against each other on all goods because one country's
exports are another's imports.

In a later empirical paper, Jan Wszelaki has argued that the bloc countries were held "captive" by their dependence on the Soviet Union for raw materials.[51] His figures also showed price discrimination by the Soviet monopoly.

Ostensibly, the period when the trade between the two areas was conducted at Soviet-imposed "special" prices was closed in 1957. Yet, Soviet trade data indicates that the Soviet Union has continued to underpay for its imports from and to overcharge for its exports to the captive area, in comparison with the prices prevailing in its trade with Western Europe and other parts of the Free World. Indeed, Soviet trade statistics show that the overpayment by the captive area for Soviet export goods has more than tripled between 1957-1959.[52]

Laszlo Zsoldos attempted to test the claim that world market prices present a relevant criterion on which to measure discrimination.[53] Zsoldos's analysis is very limited by the size of his sample. Using Hungarian data, he calculated average unit values for six export commodities and seven import categories. He used these data to measure changes in the unit values through time and differences in the unit values between areas at one point in time. Zsoldos concluded that Hungary buys above world market prices from the bloc and the West. Western imports are even higher priced than the bloc imports. This discrimination, Zsoldos argued, is a result of the infrequency and bilateral nature of Hungarian transactions. He also concluded that in the absence of "regular and frequent" transactions, trade will be carried out above the world market price.

Aleksander Kutt, using Soviet data, was adamant in his accusation of Soviet wrongdoing in bloc trade.[54] He charged that in 1961, "as in previous years," the Soviet Union overpriced its exports to the bloc nations. In similar fashion, the bloc nations were underpaid for their exports to the Soviet Union. These charges were based on comparisons with similar transactions between the USSR and Western Europe. Kutt claimed that for 1961,

. . . on balance, the Soviet price discrimination on comparative sample commodities covering 58.7 percent of Soviet exports to the captive countries, amounted to 490.3 [million] export rubles, or $544.8 million.[55]

In his comprehensive study of communist trade, Frederic Pryor tested two hypotheses.[56] Examining data from Bulgaria,

Hungary, Poland, and the Soviet Union, Pryor tested the propositions
that (1) the greater the degree of dependence, the greater the discrimination, and (2) the greater the degree of monopoly power (measured by the ratio of "singly" supplied imports), the more able to
tie and therefore the more able to discriminate.* Pryor found that
trade discrimination was linked to dependence factors. In testing
his second hypothesis, "the monopoly hypothesis," he found more
difficulty because of the problems involved in determining the degree
to which the Soviet Union is a single supplier. Pryor rejected the
monopoly hypothesis. [57]

Pryor's work deserves further mention because he was the first
to point out that the price deviations could cancel each other out.
For this reason, he analyzed import and export prices (average unit
values) together by means of trade indexes. Following this procedure,
he determined if the nation was relatively discriminated against.
Pryor found the results surprising. "First, they are a good deal
more consistent from year to year than one would have suspected;
Second, the relative order** seems somewhat strange."[58] Pryor
concluded, from his investigation, that, in spite of the persistent
public claims of "proletarian internationalism," price discrimination
was the order of business.

Heinz Kohler calculated the net barter terms of trade in order
to determine if the Soviet Union has shifted exploitation from open
reparations to commercial discrimination. [59] In examining the data,
he concluded that

> . . . it seems to this author, even cautiously interpreting
> the data, that it is quite likely that the Soviet Union,
> between 1954 and 1956, has shifted exploitation to the
> commercial realm. . . . [60]

In his extremely detailed work, Alan Brown empirically in-
vestigated Hungarian data. [61] He showed, using these data, that the
country paid lower prices to the East than to the West for the same

---

*These two questions are very similar—the more the state
trading monopoly is a single supplier, the greater is the degree of
dependence its trading partners will have on it.

**For 1958, Pryor's order of decreasing discrimination runs
as follows: Hungary, Czechoslovakia, Poland, Rumania, Bulgaria,
East Germany.

goods. On the export side, he argued that Hungary received higher prices in the East for comparable commodities.

> In 1950, . . . Hungary could have obtained the Western bill of goods from the East at 74 percent of the actual prices paid to the West. On the export side, they could have sold in the East the goods which were exported to the West at 25 percent higher prices . . . in 1960, Western imports would have cost 6 percent more if purchased in the East, and Western exports would have sold at about 40 percent higher prices in Eastern trade. [62]

Brown also showed that, as Hungary increased her trade with one Eastern country, this increase led to a subsequent deterioration in the relative terms of trade with that same region.

In the final empirical investigation discussed here, P. J. D. Wiles calculates the relative terms of trade, à la Pryor. [63] He argued that East European trade necessarily contains "micro-discrimination, " but not necessarily "macro-discrimination. "*

> A high price of exports is met by a high price of imports. The temptation to export a lot to the partner offering high prices is offset by the cost of having to import as much from him at equally high prices. [64]**

He argued that the exploitation cannot be mutual. However, it can be absent altogether if the differentials balance out. To clarify his point, he pointed out that a Czechoslovak official might complain about the high price of Russian timber vis-à-vis Swedish timber, but he forgets that Czech export prices to Russia are equally high. Wiles, in concluding, recognized that these differentials might not balance out and that this would mean one country would "profit" at the expense of the other. He does not believe that these deviations are the result of the price discrimination because of monopoly power. He argued,

---

*Wiles argues that the prices per item may give evidence of discrimination, but the deviations may cancel on the entire trade package.

**By the nature of bilateral agreements, a country must import from the country it exports to.

. . . if my view is right, a Prebisch-Popovic type of aid
through trade is practiced, not commodity by commodity,
but country by country; and it is this principle that gov-
erns the deviations from world prices within the CMEA. [65]

In summarizing this literature we are reminded by the comments
of Lynn Turgeon, in his recent book, that the discussion begun by
Mendershausen is still very much a part of the literature. [66] Turgeon
agrees with Holzman that these losses are simply a reflection of
bloc autarky. He feels the growing trade with Western Europe will
reduce such losses as the bloc autarky breaks down. Turgeon feels
that the Western traders will not trade with the Russians unless a
little "sweetening is added. " "Thus, the differential shown by Mendershausen and Kutt is, at least partly, a reflection of higher profits
for West European importers and exporters, as a result of this
lucrative price discrimination in their favor. "[67]

The reviewed studies present two opposing positions. On the
one hand we have the hypothesis presented by Mendershausen, Kutt,
Wszelaki, and Pryor that these deviations are the manifestation
of the monopoly power of trading monopolies. The contention is
that these deviations represent price discrimination. A quite different
view is presented by Holzman and Wiles. In his customs union
argument, Holzman states that, in any preferential group, prices
will, indeed should, differ. * Wiles has argued that this group of
nations practice an aid through trade system of price differentials.**

In the context of these differing views, we will examine the
Yugoslav experience in an attempt to distinguish the effects of Yugoslav
state trading with the Comecon nations.

Such a study was suggested by a preliminary examination carried
out in the manner of Mendershausen's work. The aggregate data
on Yugoslav exports and imports were calculated to yield "average
unit values. " These "average unit values" were calculated by dividing
the dinar value of the exports (imports) to (from) a country by the

---

*He does not argue that these differentiated prices represent
a cost to some members and a profit to others.

**If the countries are forced by the monopoly power of the
Soviet Union to enter in this aid program, it represents a type of
discrimination.

quantity exported (imported) in tons. This produced the average
value per ton (or other measure of quantity), which was taken to
represent the price charged per ton. These prices could then be
compared.

In dealing with the broadest part of this investigation, comparison
of the average prices charged the Eastern and Western trading partners, "average unit values" were calculated for twelve export categories and thirteen import categories. Average unit values were
then calculated for four years (1964-67) within each category. This
allowed detection of movements within the categories, as well as a
comparison between them.

On the export side of the trading figures, the data indicated
that Yugoslavia charged the Eastern bloc countries a higher price
than the Western European countries in 27 of the 48 instances (56
percent). The movements over time indicated that this relationship
did not change to any degree over the four-year period. If Yugoslavia
charged the West European countries a higher price for the commodity than she did the East European nations, this relationship was
maintained over the period.

There was, however, a slight trend toward higher average
unit values for the Eastern customers. In 1964 and 1965, Yugoslavia
charged the Eastern nations higher prices for 6 of the 13 commodities,
in 1966, for 7 of the 13 commodities, and in 1967, for 8 of the 13
commodities.

Few, if any, conclusions can be drawn from these general
data.* These results do not conform to the results Mendershausen
and Holzman calculated for Russia and Bulgaria.** In defense of the
technique it should be pointed out that the assumption about quality
differences may be the cause of some of the inconsistencies. If
Yugoslavia exports its highest quality goods to the West and still

------

*If for no other reason, the results are tenuous because the
commodity categories are unweighted as to their relative importance
in the export bundle. The Mendershausen-Holzman studies suffer
from this same problem.

**For example, Mendershausen shows higher average unit
values for 41 out of the 49 commodities Russia sold the bloc countries in 1958.

charges the East a high price, this only results in understating the "discrimination." However, if she exports inferior goods to the East and charges the East a lower price than the West, there still may be discrimination. She may be charging the Eastern customers a higher price than she would charge the Western customers for these inferior goods. The dilemma is that, instead of showing up as "discrimination" against the Eastern nations, in this study such action shows up as discrimination by the Eastern nations.* It seems valid to argue that, to the extent that the commodity classifications have quality differences, they understate the discriminatory power of the state trading monopoly.**

The import side of these calculations is even less meaningful. The quality difference of goods imported from different countries is likely to be substantial. In this case, the monopoly power should manifest itself in higher prices paid to the West European countries than to the East European countries. In this case, the inferior goods argument cuts the opposite way. If Yugoslavia imports inferior goods from the East, it should overstate the discrimination by lowering the "average unit values." The results of these calculations seem to confirm this fact. In 44 of the 52 instances (87 percent), Yugoslavia paid higher prices for the commodities she bought from the West.***

---

*It shows up as higher "average unit values" on free markets, reflecting (supposedly) strong Comecon bargaining.

**This is only true if the inferior goods are exported to the Eastern trading partners, which Professor A. Bajt felt to be the case. This will be discussed in greater detail in a later section.

***These figures are suspicious in that the large disparity in prices might indicate that Yugoslavia is buying different products within the commodity category. This would seem to be more likely in the case of imports than of exports. The export figures did not deviate as far from each other as did the import figures. This problem will be partially overcome later by the available data classified according to the SITC (Standard International Trade Classification). This statistical evidence will not be presented, as more complete findings will be reported later.

These data do not conclusively substantiate the hypothesis in the manner of the Mendershausen and Holzman studies. Like the previous studies, they suffer from many problems. There does, however, seem to be some evidence in support of the contention that Yugoslavia's state trading monopoly is successful in discriminating against the Eastern bloc nations. As we will see below, it is possible to use more comprehensive data in a more complete calculation in order to examine the effects of the Yugoslav state trading monopoly.

NOTES

1.   Jacob Viner, Trade Relations Between Free-Market and Controlled Economies (Geneva: League of Nations, 1943), and "International Relations Between State-Controlled National Economies, " American Economic Review, XXIV (March 1944), 315-29.

2.   Viner, Trade Relations, p. 81.

3.   Viner, "International Relations, " p. 320.

4.   Wassily Leontief, "The Pure Theory of Guaranteed Annual Wage Contract, " Journal of Political Economy, LIV (February 1946), 76-77.

5.   "Yugoslavs Outline Soviet Monopoly," New York Times, April 24, 1950, p. 5.

6.   Edward Ames, "International Trade Without Markets, " American Economic Review, XLIV (December 1954), 791-807.

7.   Nicolas Spulber and Franz Gehrels, "The Operation of Trade Within the Soviet Bloc, " Review of Economics and Statistics, XL (May 1958), 144.

8.   John Hazard, "State Trading in History and Theory," Law and Contemporary Problems, XXIV (Spring 1959), 241-55.

9.   "Trade Policy Quandry, " New York Times, December 2, 1958, p. 17.

10.   Don Humphrey, "The Economic Consequences of State Trading, " Law and Contemporary Problems, XXIV (Spring 1959), 276-90.

11. J. E. S. Fawcett, "State Trading and International Organization," Law and Contemporary Problems, XXIV (Spring 1959), 341-47.

12. Nicolas Spulber, "The Soviet-Bloc Foreign Trade System," Law and Contemporary Problems, XXIV (Summer 1959), 420-34.

13. Ibid., p. 430.

14. Robert Loring Allen, Soviet Economic Warfare (Washington: Public Affairs Press, 1960).

15. Ibid., p. 27.

16. Frederic L. Pryor, "Foreign Trade Theory in the Communist Bloc," Soviet Studies, XIV (July 1962), 41-61, and The Communist Foreign Trade System (Cambridge, Mass.: The MIT Press, 1963).

17. Pryor, The Communist Foreign Trade System, p. 132.

18. Ibid., p. 131.

19. Ibid., p. 135.

20. P. J. D. Wiles, Communist International Economics (New York: Praeger, 1969), p. 240.

21. Ibid., p. 136.

22. Ibid., p. 137.

23. Ibid., p. 138.

24. Ibid., p. 139.

25. Sidney Dell, Trade Blocs and Common Markets (New York: Alfred A. Knopf, 1963).

26. Gottfried Haberler, "Theoretical Reflections on the Trade of Socialist Economies," in Alan Brown and Egon Neuberger, eds., International Trade and Central Planning (Los Angeles: The University of California Press, 1968).

27. Oscar Lange, "On the Economic Theory of Socialism," in On the Economic Theory of Socialism, ed., Benjamin E. Lippincott (Minneapolis: University of Minnesota Press, 1938).

88   YUGOSLAVIA'S FOREIGN TRADE

28. H. D. Dickinson, Economics of Socialism (London: Oxford University Press, 1937), p. 173n.

29. Haberler, "Theoretical Reflections," p. 31.

30. G. Warren Nutter, "Trends in Eastern Europe," Economic Age, November-December 1968, pp. 8-12.

31. Ibid., p. 12.

32. Jan M. Michal, "Czechoslovakia's Foreign Trade," Slavic Review, XXVII (June 1968), 212-29.

33. Horst Mendershausen, "Terms of Trade Between the Soviet Union and Smaller Communist Countries, 1955-57," and "The Terms of Soviet-Satellite Trade: A Broadened Analysis," both in Review of Economics and Statistics, May 1959 and May 1960, respectively. Also see the original RAND studies for complete texts of the papers.

34. Horst Mendershausen, The Terms of Soviet-Satellite Trade: 1955-1959, RM-2507 (Santa Monica: The RAND Corporation, March 1960), p. 4.

35. Ibid., p. 10.

36. Ibid., p. 11.

37. Ibid., p. 16.

38. Ibid.

39. Ibid., taken from Academiia Nauk SSSR, Institut Economiki, Politicheskaia Ekonomiia, 3d ed., rev. (Moscow, 1958), pp. 660-61.

40. Ibid., p. 28.

41. Franklyn D. Holzman, "Soviet Trade Pricing and the Question of Discrimination," Review of Economics and Statistics, May 1962, pp. 134-47.

42. V. Kaigl in Pryor, "Foreign Trade Theory," p. 56.

43. Franklyn Holzman, "More on Soviet Bloc Trade Discrimination," Soviet Studies, XVII (July 1965), 44-65.

44. Ibid., p. 50.

45. Ibid., p. 52.

46. Ibid., p. 56.

47. Horst Mendershausen, "Mutual Price Discrimination in Soviet Bloc Trade," and "A Final Comment," and Franklyn D. Holzman, "Soviet Bloc Mutual Discrimination: Comment," all in Review of Economics and Statistics, XLIV, November 1962.

48. Mendershausen, "Mutual Price Discrimination," p. 493.

49. Ibid.

50. Mendershausen, "A Final Comment," p. 499.

51. Jan Wszelaki, "Economic Developments in East Central Europe, 1954-1959," Orbis, IV (Winter 1961), 422-23.

52. Ibid., p. 434.

53. Laszlo Zsoldos, Economic Integration of Hungary into the Soviet Bloc (Columbus: The Ohio State University Press, 1963).

54. Aleksander Kutt, "Prices and the Balance Sheet in Soviet-Captive Countries' Trade in 1960," Report Presented to the Assembly of Captive European Nations General Committee, December, 343 (April 1963), pp. 83-100.

55. Ibid., p. 85.

56. Pryor, The Communist Foreign Trade System.

57. For a detailed exposition of his methods and results, see ibid., pp. 144-53.

58. Ibid., p. 146.

59. Heinz Kohler, Economic Integration in the Soviet Bloc (New York: Praeger, 1965).

60. Ibid., p. 358. Emphasis is his.

61. Alan Brown, "The Economics of Centrally Planned Foreign

Trade: The Hungarian Experience" (unpublished Ph. D. dissertation, Harvard University, 1966).

62. Ibid., p. 221.

63. P. J. D. Wiles, Communist International Economics.

64. Ibid., p. 227.

65. Ibid., p. 247.

66. Lynn Turgeon, The Contrasting Economics (Boston: Allyn and Bacon, 1969).

67. Ibid., p. 348.

6

YUGOSLAVIA
AND
STATE TRADING

The Yugoslav position enables us to study the effects of state trading more thoroughly than in any of the previously mentioned studies. Many of the glaring inadequacies of these studies can be overcome in examining the case of Yugoslavia. We will begin with a discussion of the data. Next, a model will be developed that will be used in analyzing the Yugoslav data. We will then present and analyze the Yugoslav evidence. In concluding, the results will be discussed further and the conclusions summarized. An exhibit containing the evidence gathered appears in an appendix.

THE DATA

Perhaps the most serious charge that can be leveled against all of the previous empirical studies concerns the data used. Although the trade data of the Eastern European countries are probably the most reliable of the statistics they report, they suffer from not being classified according to the SITC (Standard International Trade Classification). (They are reliable in that the exports [imports] are imports [exports] of another country and can, therefore, be cross-checked. The U.N. reports that "A comparison between Eastern and Western European trade statistics yields a satisfactorily high correspondence.")[1] As a result of their not being classified, one can never be certain that the commodity groups being compared are the same. If they are, the measured differentials may not be price discrimination, but rather price differentials resulting from the sale of different commodities. Not only are the commodity groups unclassified, but also they are very broad groupings. As a result, there is room for

very much diversity within the category.* The Yugoslav data, while
still subject to some of these same weaknesses, are broken down in
more detail. Yugoslavia reports all trade statistics in a Foreign
Trade Annual Classified according to the Standard International Trade
Classification.** These data are reported by country of sale or purchase in quantity and value amounts for all items.[2] This allows the
calculation of average unit values for fine categories of commodities.
Not only is the homogeneity assumption much more valid, but the
classifications are the same for both the East and the West.

Holzman argued that if the Eastern nations are discriminated
against by the West, i.e., if export prices to the East are higher than
"world market prices" and import prices from the East are lower
than "world market prices," it would show up as mutual bloc discrimination. Zsoldos has argued that these differentials exist and are a
result of the infrequency of East European transactions on the markets
of West Europe. Again, in the case of Yugoslavia, this will not be a
problem. Yugoslavia has purposely integrated into the markets of
Western Europe to the point of restructuring her institutional mechanism. We should find little of this Western "discrimination" against
Yugoslavia.***

---

*For example, Mendershausen calculates an average unit value
for the commodity paper products. Paper products, if classified
according to the Standard International Trade Classification, would
be broken down into 32 items.

**The Standard International Trade Classification, a 5-digit
classifying system, breaks down the commodities traded into 1,312
separate items. Yugoslavia further separates commodities by adding
two additional digits. This greatly increases the fine breakdown of
the classifying system and adds validity to the homogeneity assumption
that will be necessary in examining the data.

***In the empirical work that follows, unit values received and
paid by Yugoslavia will be the actual unit values. We will be revaluing
the export and import bundles traded with Eastern Europe at prices
Yugoslavia could receive and pay on Western markets. This will
circumvent the question of Western discrimination which would be
caused by using "prices on Western markets."

A MODEL OF STATE TRADING

This chapter has been dealing with the exploitative effects of state trading. We will proceed with an attempt to measure the discriminatory power of the Yugoslav trading monopoly. Before proceeding any further, it is necessary to examine what is meant by discrimination. The term discrimination, which has been used profusely in previous studies, is not easy to pin down.[3] The theorists' model of simple price discrimination requires the monopolist to separate his markets according to their demand elasticities, adjusting quantities sold in each so as to equate marginal revenues. This definition of discrimination is quite different from the definition of discrimination in international trade literature. In fact, according to the Havana Charter for the International Trade Organization, a country can absolve itself of a charge of discrimination by showing it sells in the highest price market.[4] Discrimination, in this case, means the transaction of trade based on considerations other than purely economic considerations. Thus, discrimination could be demonstrated in court by evidence that imports were not purchased from the country quoting the lowest price.

Holzman discusses the blurring of these definitions in his "Discrimination in International Trade."[5] Consider three countries: A, B, and C. A places quantitative restrictions on imports from B, but not from C. Therefore, A's importers are paying a higher price on imports from C than these imports would cost in B. Holzman says that in this case, the reverse of traditional price discrimination, A has provided the separation of markets necessary for C to practice price discrimination over her own importers. In his second explanation of discrimination, Holzman draws an analogy to the bilateralism practiced by Germany in the 1930s. In this case it would be argued that A forced its importers to pay the higher-than-market price in order to extract a more than compensating premium on her exports to C. This second explanation is relevant to our examination of the effects of state trading. Because of the bilateral nature of the intra-bloc trade, it is necessary to calculate a type of "net discrimination." Wiles calls attention to this fact in distinguishing between micro- and macro-discrimination.[6] He argues that the micro-discrimination is immediately apparent, but "The prevailing bilateralism makes the process mutual. So there is not necessarily any macro-discrimination in the terms or direction of trade."[7] The lack of this macro-discrimination is claimed by communist leaders. In a typical statement, Wladyslaw Gomulka argues,

If, under the method of firm prices applied in trade between
our countries for periods of one or two years, coal prices
in trade with the USSR were somewhat lower than coal prices
on other markets, then correspondingly, the prices of some
goods delivered to Poland by the Soviet Union were lower
than prices on the world market. This concerns, for example, iron ores, textiles, and ships. (The difference in the
price of iron ore even amounted to several dollars [per ton]
compared to the price of ores of the same quality on other
markets.) For equilibrating the price deviation on coal,
other Polish goods were sold to the Soviet Union at prices
higher than the price on world markets. (The price of wool
cloth exported to the Soviet Union, in the amount of approximately 5,000,000 meters, was higher by 5-6 rubles a meter
in comparison with the prices at which we could sell this
cloth on markets.) This means that the basic agreement
reached by the Ministries of Foreign Trade was based on
the level of world prices. If both sides agreed to some deviations for particular goods, the principle in settling accounts was the following: The sum of the deviations above
and below must be mutually equal so that neither side would
suffer loss.[8]

The possibility of such balancing makes it necessary to measure
these deviations in order to determine the level of macro-discrimination.

The institutional framework of the bloc countries makes the
measurement of these deviations necessary. The state trading monopoly of one bloc country bargains with the state monopoly of another.
The solution is indeterminate and is decided by sheer bargaining
power. In this case, however, there is more than the analysis of
bilateral monopoly. The monopolists are constrained by the fact that
they must buy as much as they sell. Yugoslavia sells her exports
to the bloc countries through bilateral negotiations at a higher price
than these exports could command on world markets. However,
these transactions are in turn, bilateral. All the exchange earnings
these exports receive must be spent on exports from that same
country, which in turn, are purchased at a price which is above the
world market price. The power to practice price discrimination
will be found after all these deviations are netted out.

The important point is to discover the net gain (or loss) brought
about by the ability of the state trading monopoly to discriminate.
Suppose Yugoslavia exports wheat to the Soviet Union and imports

vodka from the Soviet Union. Prices are bargained by the state monopolies, and the total value of trade, over the period covered by the
negotiations, must balance bilaterally. Yugoslavia could sell and buy
these products on Western markets for $2 per bushel and $3 per
bottle, respectively. If, at the end of the trading period, we find that
Yugoslavia has sold 100 bushels of wheat to the Soviet Union for $4
per bushel and purchased 100 bottles of vodka at $4 per bottle, the
trade is bilaterally balanced. We do, however, have price discrimination.* Yugoslavia was able to receive 33-1/3 more bottles of vodka
by dealing through the state trading monopoly. The monopoly has ex-
tracted a $100 "profit" from the state trading monopoly of the Soviet
Union.** In order to determine the power of one state monopoly vis-
à-vis another it will be necessary to extend such an analysis to cover
the commodities actually exchanged by the bloc countries. In order
to avoid such further entanglement concerning the use of the word
discrimination, I will call this "net discrimination" the monopoly
profit (loss) of state trading.***

Yugoslavia earns revenue from her exports to the East and West.
Her imports from the East and West cause payments to leave the Yugoslav economy. We can, therefore, calculate whether the Comecon
trade represented a net profit or loss in terms of what this trade
would have earned and cost on Western markets. For each good exported we have revenue received from trade with the Soviet Union
above (below) what this good would have earned on Western markets.
This will be represented by $TR_{x_r} - TR_{x_w}$ where TR_{x_w} is the total
revenue received from the sale of good x on Western markets. We

---

*This would be Wiles's macro-discrimination.

**In effect we are determining how much the Soviet Union would
have to pay for the same bundle of goods purchased on the world
market.

***This is analogous to Wiles's macro-discrimination and Pryor's
combined import and export trade indices. If a bloc country, by en-
gaging in state trading, gains a monopoly profit through this trade,
the trade index moved over 100 percent; it is guilty of macro-price
discrimination. This measure is, however, distinct from Pryor's
calculations of the relative price discrimination of the USSR between
the bloc nations. It measures the absolute price discrimination of
the Yugoslav state monopoly against the communist countries, using
free market prices as a standard.

can call this "monopoly revenue" the MA (Market Advantage of State Trading). As pointed out above, for each good imported we have a cost above what the good would cost on Western markets. This will be represented by $TC_{y_r} - TC_{y_w}$ when TC_{y_r} is the cost of importing good Y from Russia and TCy_w is what the cost of importing Y from Western exporters would be. This excess cost of Comecon trade can be represented by MD (Market Disadvantage). By calculating the MA for goods 1 . . . n and the MD for goods 1 . . . m, we can obtain a net profit or cost of Yugoslavia's trade with the Soviet Union.* If MA = MD, then the Gomulka argument quoted above would be substantiated. But if MA > MD, then the Yugoslav state trading monopoly has price discriminated against the Soviet Union. If MA < MD, the Soviet state monopoly has proved to be the stronger in the bilateral negotiations.

In algebraic terms we are calculating π, the gain or loss of trading with the Comecon countries via the state trading monopoly.** This is done separately for each bloc country. The algebraic model for the case of trade with the Soviet Union will be presented below. The equations for the other countries would be identical after altering superscripts. The price of the export is calculated from value and quantity data $P_j^{xr} = V_j^{xr} / Q_j^{xr}$. Where P_j^{xr} = the export price of good j to the Soviet Union; Q_j^{xr} = the quantity of good j exported to the Soviet Union; V_j^{xr} = the money value of Q_j^{xr}. Similarly, $P_j{}^{xw}$ is the price that the Yugoslav export (good j) could have commanded on Western markets. Using these figures we can calculate the expression $Q_j^{xr} (P_j^{xr} - P_j^{xw})$ which represents the dinar advantage of exporting good (j) to the Soviet Union rather than to Western markets. The import disadvantage is calculated in the same manner: $Q_k^{mr} (P_k^{mr} - P_k^{mw})$, represents the cost of importing from the Soviet Union instead of Western markets.*** The two expressions are combined and summed over the entire range of exports (1 . . . n) and imports (1 . . . m) to give us π.

---

*This can be calculated for all Eastern European countries and the combination would represent a net profit cost of Comecon trade in toto.

**This gain or loss will be the definition of discrimination for this study.

***Where Q_k^{mr} = quantity of import K from the Soviet Union; V_k^{mr} = money value of Q_k^{mr}; $P_k^{mr} = V_k^{mr} / Q_k^{mr}$.

$$\pi = \sum_{j=1}^{n} Q_j^{xr} (P_j^{xr} - P_j^{xw}) - \sum_{k=1}^{m} Q_k^{mr} (P_k^{mr} - P_k^{mw}).*$$

This formula will be used to determine what in fact the Yugoslav state trading monopoly gains from such trade.

THE YUGOSLAV EVIDENCE

The procedure outlined above was applied to Yugoslav data for the three year period, 1966-68. The results are presented below. In making the actual calculations, for the sake of economy, any export or import items that accounted for less than 300,000 dinars of trade were ignored.** This enabled the discarding of approximately

---

*As discussed above, if $\pi > 0$ the Yugoslav foreign trade monopoly was able to profit (price discriminate) in dealing with her Soviet equivalent. If $\pi < 0$, the opposite is true, and if $\pi = 0$ the Soviet and Yugoslav foreign trade monopolies operate on the principle of selfless mutual support, which so often is claimed by Soviet sources. Because the raw data are in the form V_j^{xw}, Q_j^{xw}, etc., it simplifies the expression to calculate $\pi = \sum_{j=1}^{n} (V_j^{xr}) - [V_j^{xw}/Q_j^{xw} (Q_j^{xr})] - \sum_{k=1}^{m}$
$(V_r^{mr}) - [V_k^{mw}/Q_r^{mw} (Q_r^{mr})]$. This expression makes it clear that we are revaluing the Eastern bundle of goods at Western prices. This simplification will be carried out in the following section which deals with actual calculations.

**Originally, sampling techniques were to be applied to the data in an effort to reduce the number of calculations. Applying the sampling techniques proved to be unfruitful because the great differences in the size (value) of the items produced too large a variance to allow satisfactory results. Solving this problem by sampling the percentage discrimination per item produced a mean percentage discrimination that was unacceptable because it was unweighted by the differing value importances of the items. The procedure of dropping those items with a value of under 300,000 dinars was then employed because it enabled a great saving in time expenditure with very little loss in the value of the results. Exact figures as to the size of the sample are presented in Appendix C.

75 percent of the seven-digit categories with only a small loss of the total dinar value of trade.

In proceeding with the analysis it was assumed that the seven-digit categories were fine enough to ensure one item per category. Additionally, it was assumed that the quality of all the items within the category was homogeneous.*

The data on exports are reported f.o.b. (freight on board) and therefore required no assumption concerning transport and insurance costs. Imports are reported c.i.f. (cost, insurance, and freight). Accordingly, we must assume that the transportation costs on all items within a category are equal. Such costs would then have negligible effect on the unit value comparisons.**

The data reported in Statistika Spoljne Trgovine SFR Jugoslavije were used to compute the average unit values of each item which met the criteria of having over 300,000 dinars of trade.*** The Western price was calculated using this same data source and taking a weighted mean of unit values from (to) the three most important sources (buyers) of the item.**** The results, therefore, measure the gain

---

*It was previously argued that this assumption is much more realistic for the Yugoslav data than for any previous data. This assumption can be dropped if we assume that any quality differences are randomly distributed without regard to the political color of the trading partner. The assumption of quality homogeneity concerning export items is most probably more valid. In regard to import items, it is very suspicious. The effects of these quality differences on the measured degree of discrimination will be discussed in Chapter 7.

**In an effort to make this assumption credible, the "free-market price" was calculated as a "Western-Europe price." This differs from previous studies that included imports from the United States in the "free-market" calculations. Western-Europe prices were used to make transportation costs (etc.) the same (roughly) on an item imported from the bloc or the West.

***See Appendix C for a more detailed explanation of the selection criteria and a presentation of the data.

****Yugoslavia enjoys MFN treatment in West European markets. This unique Yugoslav situation diminished Holzman's argument of Western discrimination.

accruing to Yugoslavia from state trading. This profit is measured
on the basis of the Western price, and we are implicitly assuming
that if Yugoslavia so chose she could import (export) these additional
items from (to) Western Europe at the prevailing price.

In effect, we are arguing that Yugoslavia's share of the Western
market is so small as to have negligible effect on the prices on this
market. The evidence indicates this to be the case. Kaser argues
that all of Comecon together would have no effect on Western prices,

> Even if Comecon were to act as a common negotiator in
> each of the Western European trading groups (a function
> it is unlikely to fill despite occasional such hopes chiefly
> expressed in Hungary), it would have greatly to expand its
> sales in the West in order to influence prices. During
> 1959-65 it sold a steady 7 percent of its exports to EEC
> and an equally steady 6 percent to EFTA; in 1965, these
> were a mere 2.8 percent of total EEC imports, 4.0 per-
> cent of EFTA imports, and 2.9 percent of OECD imports.[9]

The results in Table 16 demonstrate that Yugoslavia was indeed
a net gainer from the state trading. Yugoslavia discriminated against
the bloc countries in both the export and import package. The export overcharge, however, was not nearly as great as the import
underpayment. These results clearly negate the Wiles argument
discussed above.* In all import instances, Yugoslavia received the
bundle of goods for a lower price than a like bundle would have cost
on Western markets. Likewise, on all but 8 of the 24 export bundles,
the exception being exports to the Soviet Union (all three years), and
exports to Bulgaria, Czechoslovakia, East Germany, Hungary, and
Rumania in 1966, Yugoslavia was able to charge the bloc nations a
higher price than a similar bundle would have commanded on Western
markets. In no instance did the differentials "cancel out," producing
no "macro-discrimination." The result of combining the two indicates
that Yugoslavia, in her trade with the bloc nations, gained a monopoly
profit amounting to 28.8 percent (over the three-year period) of the
trade turnover revalued at Western prices. The country breakdown
shows the range of the results.

---

*See pp. 81 - 82. It is not meaningful to examine the export
and import bundle separately because of the bilateral nature of the
trade. The only reason for separating the two is to examine the Wiles-
Gomulka argument.

TABLE 16

Gain or Loss in Trade with Comecon, 1966-68*
(value in thousands of dinars)

Country	1966	1967	1968
Albania	101,004	123,760	126,172
Bulgaria	189,122	99,954	173,432
Czechoslovakia	730,942	865,383	1,619,171
E. Germany	460,471	499,704	598,674
Hungary	405,382	308,686	597,925
Poland	900,652	439,093	388,583
Rumania	465,034	227,130	272,016
USSR	1,045,333	795,327	1,591,376

$$*\pi = \sum_{j=1}^{n} Q_j^{xr} (P_j^{xr} - P_j^{xw}) - \sum_{k=1}^{m} Q_k^{mr} (P_k^{mr} - P_k^{mw}).$$

Source: See Table A-6, Appendix A.

In combining the export and import prices, in order to calculate the "macro-discrimination," we find that Yugoslavia was able to profit by "dealing" with Comecon from 1966 to 1968, by the amount of 13.02 billion dinars. This represents a gain of 28.8 percent over what these goods could have earned and would have cost if traded on Western Markets. The country breakdown on the total trade turnover for the three-year period ranges from a gain of 20 percent to 71 percent. Table 17 arrays the varying levels of discrimination over the three-year period. The USSR, Bulgaria, and East Germany fare better than the all-Comecon standard, while Poland, Czechoslovakia, Hungary, and Rumania do worse. Albania is discriminated to such a degree as to be in a unique situation. When the Soviet Union is excluded from the Comecon average, the level of discrimination increases significantly (from 28.8 percent to 34.2 percent).

Separating the country breakdown into yearly changes allows us to witness some movements in the levels of discrimination (Figure 2). The trend appears to be toward increased discrimination (Market Advantage) on the part of Yugoslavia. The 1968 levels are above the levels for the entire three-year period. Poland and Rumania are the two exceptions to this trend. The relative position of the

TABLE 17

Market Advantage (Discrimination) of
Yugoslav Trade with Comecon, 1966-68

Countries	Gain as Percent of Revalued (Western Price) Trade Package*
USSR	20.0
Bulgaria	21.6
E. Germany	25.5
All Comecon	28.8
Poland	32.5
All Comecon (except USSR)	34.2
Czechoslovakia	38.8
Hungary	39.6
Rumania	41.1
Albania	71.0

$$* \sum_{j=1}^{n} Q_j^{xr} (P_j^{xr} - P_j^{xw}) - \sum Q_k^{mr} (P_k^{mr} - P_k^{mw}) / \sum_{j=1}^{n} Q_j^{xr} P_j^{xw} + \sum_{k=1}^{m} Q_k^{mr} P_k^{mw}$$

Source: Appendix C; Table C-2. See C-2 for dinar figures of discrimination.

countries within the discrimination hierarchy while changing, exhibits stability. With the notable exception of Czechoslovakia, there seems to be a quite stable hierarchy of levels of discrimination. This stability is consistent with earlier investigations.*

It is interesting to compare the relative arrangements of the countries within the discrimination hierarchy to the resulting arrangements in other studies. Pryor remarks on the stability of the positions over time as he measures the relative bargaining position of the bloc countries vis-à-vis the Soviet Union. In order of decreasing bargaining position in 1957, Pryor lists East Germany, Bulgaria, Poland, Rumania, Czechoslovakia, and Hungary.[10]

---

*The significant increase in the level of discrimination against Czechoslovakia may be the result of the political climate existing in Czechoslovakia.

FIGURE 2

Gain (Discrimination) from Yugoslav Trade
with Comecon, 1966-68

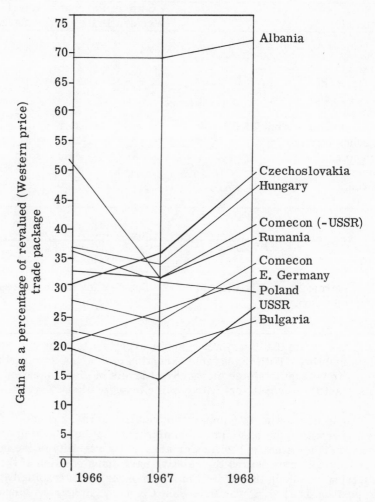

Source: Appendix C, Table C-2. See Table C-2 for dinar measures of discrimination.

102

Mendershausen, calculating discrimination on exports only for the same year, comes up with a quite different arrangement. He finds Rumania in the strongest bargaining position vis-à-vis the Soviet Union, followed in order by East Germany, Bulgaria, Poland, Hungary, Czechoslovakia, and Albania. (Mendershausen's results do not exhibit the stability of Holzman's. From 1957 to 1959 Albania moves from the most to the least discriminated against [by the USSR].)[11] It is interesting to note that when Mendershausen traces out data for particular export commodities and when these commodities include prices for Yugoslavia, the prices are lower than prices to other bloc nations, but higher than prices to Western nations.[12]

Having demonstrated that Yugoslavia does gain (discriminates) in her trade with the bloc countries, and that these measures are not inconsistent with earlier studies, it would now be useful to turn to a closer examination of these results. Chapter 7 will examine some further implication of the study.

NOTES

1. Economic Bulletin for Europe, XIX, 1 (New York: United Nations, November 1967).

2. Statistika Spoljne Trgovine SFR Jugoslavije (Belgrade: Federal Institute for Statistics).

3. For a good discussion of the problem of defining discrimination see: P. J. D. Wiles, Communist International Economics (New York: Praeger, 1969); James E. Meade, The Balance of Payments (London: Oxford University Press, 1951); and Franklyn D. Holzman, "Discrimination in International Trade," American Economic Review, December 1949.

4. Holzman, "Discrimination in International Trade," p. 1236.

5. Ibid., pp. 1233-44.

6. Wiles, Communist International Economics.

7. Ibid., p. 227.

8. Kommunist (Moscow), 1/1957, p. 106, quoted by Wiles, ibid.

9. Michael Kaser, Comecon (London: Oxford University Press, 1967), p. 176.

10. Frederic L. Pryor, The Communist Foreign Trade System (Cambridge, Mass.: The MIT Press, 1963), p. 146.

11. Horst Mendershausen, The Terms of Soviet-Satellite Trade: 1955-1959, RM-2057 (Santa Monica: The RAND Corporation, March 1960), p. 44.

12. Ibid., pp. 18-26.

7

**PRICE
DISCRIMINATION:
SOME ADDITIONAL
EVIDENCE**

This chapter will examine several arguments that might be
used to discredit the hypothesis that the deviations measured in Chapter
6 reflect monopoly power. Initially, we will examine our assumption
of quality homogeneity. In this context, the use of disaggregated
measures of price deviations to measure quality difference will be
discussed. Next, we will discuss the problem of overvalued bloc
currencies. We will then present and test a simple model of trade
dependence. This will be followed by a discussion of the Yugoslav
bargaining position.

QUALITY DIFFERENCES

Earlier, in calculating the amounts of discrimination, it was
assumed that there were no quality differences in trade with Eastern
or Western Europe.* The literature does not support this assumption. There seem to be quality differences as a result of the docu-
mented inferiority of packaging and servicing (including spare parts)
and delivery unreliability on the part of Eastern Europe "firms."
As Pryor reports:

Many of the goods which the Bloc nations delivered to
each other have been of poor quality. According to a

_____

*If it could be assumed that any quality differences were dis-
tributed randomly throughout the import bundle from Eastern Europe,
the relative price deviations would be evidence of discrimination.

Western economist, "Polish coke delivered to East
Germany was repeatedly described as substandard;
electric locomotives from the Henningsdorf plant in East
Germany soon broke down in Poland; Czech equipment for
the Elblag power plant in Poland had to be replaced
twice. Similar complaints were repeatedly registered, at
least in Poland, about the quality of iron ore and cotton,
as well as about equipment supplied by the Soviet Union;
apparently, there were attempts to sell used and recon-
ditioned Soviet equipment as new. In 1958, 2,000,000
Soviet clinical thermometers were scrapped as substandard."[1]

It might be argued that what we have labeled discrimination in
Chapter 6 may simply be price differentials reflecting quality differences. Therefore, it is worthwhile to briefly examine how some
economists have dealt with differences in quality.

Until recently there were no attempts to quantify quality differences. There have, however, been some recent investigations into
this area.

The technique of solving the problem of quality in international price comparisons is this: The application of
regression analysis to price measurements rests on the
hypothesis that price differences among variants of a
product in a particular market can be accounted for by
identifiable characteristics of these variants. By fitting
a regression equation to observations on the price and
characteristics of these commodity variants, typically
in a cross-section for a market at a given time, we can
learn which characteristics are associated with the price
of the commodity, and what the relationship is, and, if
we have properly identified the relevant characteristics,
the coefficients of the equation can be interpreted as
prices of these characteristics.[2]

This method has not (to my knowledge) been attempted on any products
in East-West trade.[3] These recent studies suggest areas for further
inquiry rather than advancing evidence for this study.

Recent empirical studies on East European trade have regarded
these quality differences with varying degrees of importance. Wiles

presents a "quality hierarchy"[4] that should work to minimize quality differences.*

> . . . an absurd "quality hierarchy" grows up: goods for home use, exports to other STE's exports to UDC's, exports to ACC's. Were it not for this hierarchy it is scarcely to be believed that any quality would be as good as it is. . . . Another rational explanation might be that the more advanced the country, the better the quality it demands. But while this may explain the difficulties felt by STE's selling to ACC's, it does not explain why these same ACC's tend to export only their best goods to each other, or why STE's sell better goods to other STE's than they use at home.[5]

Alan Brown indicates (in a footnote) an attempt to quantify quality differences in his study on Hungarian foreign trade.

> According to a pilot study, if quality differences were taken into account, the regional index of imports would be raised by about 10 percent (somewhat above 10 percent in 1950 and a little less than 10 percent in 1960), but the elimination of the more heterogeneous commodities from the index would also raise the discrimination index of exports in about the same proportion.[6]

In their studies on trade discrimination, Holzman, Marer, Mendershausen, Pryor, and Zsoldos have excluded items they felt would clearly violate homogeneity assumptions.[7] In each case the differences in the sample size varied substantially as a result of these various decision rules. L. Zsoldos's sample consists of only six export commodities and seven import categories. P. Marer, paying less attention to quality, includes many more commodities and, in turn, uses his price differentials as indicators of quality. In his study, using Hungarian and Austrian data, Marer argues that his divergent price indexes between the commodity groups probably

---

*In Wiles's notation an ACC is an advanced capitalist country; an STE is a Soviet type country; and a UDC is an underdeveloped country.

reflect quality differences.* Marer uses his indexes, showing that prices of raw materials in the bloc are close to world prices while trade in machinery shows substantial deviations from Western prices, as an indication of these quality differences. In all of these studies, no attempts were made to quantify quality differences.

In assessing the effect of quality differences on this study, the evidence supports the discrimination hypothesis. In the first place, in determining the Yugoslav position, we have not used prices on world markets as the Western standard, but rather prices Yugoslavia actually received on Western markets. This answers the Zsoldos arguments that the deviations we measured are the result of Western discrimination against the bloc (in this case, Yugoslavia).** It is, however, probable that some percentage of the observed deviations from the Western prices are legitimate quality differences. Two aspects of the observed deviations, however, support the discrimination hypothesis.

The first of these is the relative position of the countries by degree of discrimination. These positions are not what one would expect if the deviations were primarily the result of quality differences. The more developed countries, namely Czechoslovakia and East Germany, would most probably be exporting higher quality goods, yet these two countries are not the least discriminated against.*** These measured price differentials might be attributable to the fact that Yugoslavia's imports from these relatively industrialized countries consist primarily of manufactured goods and machines, which

_____

*Since bundles of goods are negotiated at one bargaining session, it is difficult to imagine that the price of individual items is significant for evaluating discrimination or quality differentials. See the following section of the chapter for a further discussion of price differentials by commodity group.

**Whether or not Yugoslavia is discriminated against by the Western nations is another question which could be answered by comparing the Western price standard calculated in this study to prices in intra-Western-European trade.

***Czechoslovakia fares worse than the mean for all Comecon and Comecon minus the USSR.

are more subject to quality differences, while the imports from other
bloc countries consist primarily of raw materials and other more
standard items. This possibility (that the measured deviations are
primarily a reflection of the quality of goods imported) suggests a
breakdown of Yugoslav imports by SITC section. Sections 0-5 of the
SITC are composed of items that are relatively free of quality differences. These Sections are: Food and Live Animals; Beverages and
Tobacco; Crude Materials, inedible, except fuels; Mineral Fuels,
Lubricants and Related Materials; Animal and Vegetable Oil and Fat;
Chemicals. Sections 6-8 are generally conceded to be relatively
more subject to quality differences. These Sections are Manufactured
Goods by Materials, Machinery and Transport Equipment, Miscellaneous Manufactured Goods. If we compared the percentage of
Yugoslavia's import bundle from each bloc country that is composed
of items from SITC Sections 6-8 (see Table D-1, Appendix D) to our
measured levels of discrimination we could test for such a correlation. This correlation, if present, would indicate that our measured
deviations reflect the importation of goods with varying degrees of
quality differences. Using the data reported in Table C-2 (Appendix
C), our measures of discrimination, and Table D-1, (Appendix D),
the contribution of Sections 6-8 of the SITC to the import bundle, a
coefficient of rank correlation was calculated to test the hypothesis
that the measured deviations are correlated with the percentage share
of less homogeneous imports. Our variables are X, the percentage
share of SITC Sections 6-8 in the import bundle of Yugoslavia, and
Y, the monopoly gain as a percentage. The null and alternative
hypothesis are

$$H_0 : p_S = 0$$

$$H_a : p_S > 0$$

The coefficient of rank correlation (r_S) is .0244. The t-score is
.115, which indicates that our r_S of .0244 is not significantly greater
than zero at any level.* Thus we do not reject the null hypothesis
that the observations on X and Y are independent.

This exercise, indicating that increased imports of goods from
categories more susceptible to quality differences is uncorrelated to

---

*t (cal) $= r_S - p_S / \sqrt{1 - r^2_S / n-2}$.

our measure of discrimination, lends evidence in support of the discrimination hypothesis.*

The second aspect of the observed deviations that supports the discrimination hypothesis is their movement over time. The measure fluctuates from year to year to a greater extent than one would expect quality differences to vary. Changes in the level of technology are made operational at a slow pace (particularly in Eastern Europe). This would lead one to expect that the measure of discrimination would be more stable if it primarily reflected changes in quality. Some of the fluctuations, however, undergo substantial shifts from year to year. In addition these measures fluctuate over the three-year period. If they primarily reflected quality difference one would expect more of a trend phenomenon, with some countries' measure of discrimination declining (those closing the quality difference gap) and some increasing (those whose relative quality is declining).

To sum up, there is likely some amount of systematic quality bias in our measures of discrimination. Yugoslavia probably exports higher quality goods to Western markets than to Comecon and imports higher quality goods from the West than from Comecon. This causes part of any quality differences to cancel out. The exportation of higher quality goods to Western markets causes our measure of discrimination to be understated, while importation of lower quality goods from the bloc leads to an overstatement. Table D-1, Appendix D, demonstrates that Sections 6, 7, and 8 of the SITC contribute a greater share to Yugoslav exports to the bloc than to Yugoslav imports from the bloc. This means that the Yugoslav export bundle is more heavily weighted with items subject to quality differences than the import bundle. This greater number of items subject to understatement works to offset the fact that the overstatement caused by the inferior quality of bloc imports is greater than the corresponding understatement on Yugoslav exports. The size of our measure of discrimination and its distribution and movement over time indicate that these quality biases, while working to make our measure less precise, do not cause irreparable harm.

---

*It would be interesting to attempt to break Sections 6, 7, and 8 of the SITC into smaller groups about which judgments about quality homogeneity could be made. These groups could then be subjected to a similar analysis to determine if they effect our measure of discrimination. Such a breakdown suggests possibilities for further work and is beyond the scope and intent of this study.

SECTION DEVIATIONS

In addition to the measures of discrimination on the entire trade package, calculations were made on the degree of profit or loss in each of the sections of the SITC. The 9 sections produced 18 different observations for each country per year. These disaggregated measures are important because of the significance of such measures in some of the other studies.[8] In these studies it was argued that the disaggregated measures reflected quality differences. Our disaggregated measures and information concerning the bargaining sessions discount the use of such measures to indicate differences in quality. Western accounts of the Comecon negotiating sessions portray them as very heated affairs that often center around price adjustments on only a few items. Thus, Marer writes

> . . . negotiating tactics center around the inclusion or
> exclusion of certain products in the commodity group
> for which price adjustments are to be agreed upon. . . .
> These negotiating tactics account for the fact that price
> concessions are frequently made in products which
> subsequently are in great demand while the price of
> goods available in sufficient supply remains high. . . ."[9]

This would suggest that the price deviations (discrimination) on any item cr group of items may be totally unrelated to that item. It further suggests that a meaningful measure must cancel these individual deviations and compare the price of the entire package. Thus, the correct measure is a measure of "macro-discrimination."*

Table D-2, Appendix D, arrays our section measures of discrimination. These section measures contribute empirical evidence to our contention of the insignificance of such measures as an indication of quality difference. The individual section measures lack the consistency that one would expect if they reflected the quality bias. The instability of the measures between countries and within

---

*Marer recognizes that the bargaining session determines which goods are going to be bargained (previous footnote), but then uses differing deviations on individual measures (primary products vs. machinery) as evidence of quality differences. We would argue that the higher relative prices charged for machines might reflect a strong bargaining position in foodstuffs and be unrelated to quality differences.

countries over time would seem to add some empirical support to the
contention that the bargaining is a very "active" process.

OVERVALUED CURRENCIES

An alternative explanation that must be examined is the contention that the unit-value deviations we measured are the result of
overvalued bloc currencies. Adherents of this explanation would con-
tend that the deviations exist because the soft-currency nation (Yugoslavia) is forced to accept low prices for exports from hard-currency
nations. The hard-currency nations pay lower prices to offset the
overvalued fixed exchange rates. Holzman shows that this argument
is false from both theoretical grounds and empirical evidence.

> On theoretical grounds, a difficulty with the exchange
> rate hypothesis is the fact that Soviet bloc exchange
> rates serve no "pricing" function, and in no sense pro-
> vide a link between internal and external prices. Prices
> in intra-bloc and east-west trade all take world prices
> as their starting points regardless of the official par
> values of the bloc nation's exchange rates. Thus one
> cannot argue, as with inconvertible western currencies,
> that internal prices of soft-currency countries are too
> high and that the discounts on these currencies reflect
> this fact. (The ruble exchange rate has, since 1961,
> been considered to equate roughly internal and external
> prices of traded goods—yet the ruble remains incon-
> vertible!) The Soviet bloc exchange rate systems are
> more nearly akin in practice to floating than fixed rates
> with foreign trade prices always adjusting more or less
> to world prices.
>   Empirically, where there are disequilibrium ex-
> change rates and some currencies are harder than others,
> trade in hard currencies is transacted at lower prices than
> trade between soft-currency countries. This implies (in
> our case) that not only should goods be exported to the
> west at lower prices than to the bloc, but in paying hard
> currency (as they do) to import from the west, prices
> should similarly be lower than in intrabloc trade.[10]

The evidence presented in Chapter 6 is not consistent with the
empirical evidence necessary to substantiate the "exchange rate

hypothesis."* Our evidence indicates discrimination by Yugoslavia on the import and export bundle with few exceptions. The evidence also indicates that there are a substantial number of items in both the import and export package that Yugoslavia exchanges at higher prices with the soft-currency countries than with the West.**

TRADE DEPENDENCE HYPOTHESIS

The primary goal of this study has been to determine if Yugoslavia discriminates against her Comecon trade partners. We have demonstrated that Yugoslavia did discriminate during the three-year period 1966-68, but the determinants of the level of discrimination have not been discussed. In this section we will present a simple model of the relationship between trade dependence and discrimination.***

There are quite likely many forces at work determining the level of discrimination in Yugoslav-Comecon trade. Political considerations, no doubt, play an important role. However, throughout this study it has been implicitly assumed that economic forces dominate. It is likely that in any bargaining session between bilateral monopolies the more powerful (economically) should obtain the most favorable position. One measure of the strength of state trading monopolies could be trade dependence. The more that the state trading monopoly of Yugoslavia is dependent on trade from the bloc countries, the less able it is to discriminate against them. Conversely, the more the bloc state trading monopoly is dependent on Yugoslavian trade, the more Yugoslavia should be able to discriminate. This suggests a trade dependency hypothesis; that the level of discrimination is a function of trade dependence (both in Yugoslavia and in Comecon).****

---

*"The exchange rate effect" would lead to export discrimination against the bloc and import discrimination in favor of the bloc.

**This evidence is consistent with the earlier empirical studies cited in Chapter 5.

***The model is necessarily simple because of the severe limitations imposed by the small number of observations.

****Pryor tests this same hypothesis.

Trade dependency of Country A on Country B can be measured by calculating the percentage of trade turnover that trade with Country B contributes to the total trade turnover of Country A.* Trade dependency of Country B on Country A is calculated in a similar fashion, trade turnover of B with A as a percent of the total turnover of B.

The trade dependency hypothesis can be tested by calculating a least squares regression of the form $Y = \alpha + B_1 \ln X_1 + B_2 \ln X_2$, where Y = the percentage level of discrimination,** and X_1 = the trade dependency of Yugoslavia vis-à-vis each Comecon country, and X_2 = the trade dependency of each Comecon country vis-à-vis Yugoslavia. The results of the regressions, one for each of the three years, are shown in Table 18.***

The results support the hypothesis that the level of discrimination was inversely related to the trade dependence of Yugoslavia on

---

*Another possible measure of dependence would be the ratio of the trade turnover with Country B to the GNP of Country A. This measure presents problems because of the lack of reliable (comparable) East European income estimates. The best measure of dependency of the state trading monopoly is trade as a percentage of turnover rather than GNP.

$$**\text{From Chapter 6,} \quad \sum_{n=1}^{n} Q_j^{xr} (P_j^{xr} - P_j^{xw}) - \sum_{k=1}^{m} Q_k^{mr}$$

$$(P_k^{mr} - P_k^{mw}) / \sum_{j=1}^{n} Q_j^{xr} P_j^{xw} + \sum_{k=1}^{m} Q_k^{mr} P_k^{mw}.$$

***The regressions were calculated from unrounded data in Table B-1, Appendix B, and trade turnover figures for the bloc countries from Yearbook of International Trade Statistics, 1968 (New York: Statistical Office of the United Nations, 1970). Figures for the total turnover of Albania in 1966, 1967, and 1968 had to be estimated from earlier figures. This was done by a simple linear projection of the average increase in trade turnover, 1960-64. The t-scores necessary for a .99 and .95 level of significance with 5 degrees of freedom are 4.032 and 2.571, respectively. A regression was also run on pooled data for the three-year period with the following results: $Y = 34.87 - 11.51 \ln X_1 + 14.48 \ln X_2$; the t-scores were (1.80) (9.12) - 6.39, 1.59, respectively, the R_2 (adjusted) was .636, the D.W. was 2.3 and the F-statistic was 24.01.

TABLE 18

Regression Results, 1966-68

Year		X_1 t-scores X_2		F-statistic	R^2 (adjusted)
1966	$Y = 49.11 - 10.54 \ln X_1 - 4.73 \ln X_2$ (2.93) (12.57)	-3.59	-0.38	7.96	.675
1967	$Y = 19.03 - 12.60 \ln X_1 + 32.46 \ln X_2$ (2.59) (14.48)	-4.86	2.24	11.96	.757
1968	$Y = 19.74 - 13.44 \ln X_1 + 45.89 \ln X_2$ (3.23) (20.48)	-4.15	2.24	8.68	.686

the bloc countries. The beta coefficients of the X_2 variable are not significant. In the one instance (1966) where an incorrect sign appears, the coefficient has an extremely low t-score (-0.38).

Though simple, this model has strong intuitive appeal. This hypothesis is also consistent with the observed pressures in a number of the Comecon countries to "open" westward. As these countries become less dependent on bloc trade, they effectively strengthen their Comecon bargaining position and become more of a net discriminator or are more able to countervail the countries that discriminate against them.*

THE YUGOSLAV POSITION

The preceding chapter demonstrated that Yugoslavia gains from her trade with the Comecon nations. We have seen that this gain is a function of Yugoslavia's trade dependence on the Comecon nations. The fact that Yugoslavia is able to gain this advantage in her trade with the Soviet Union is a somewhat surprising result. There are several possible explanations for this result. These explanations are all part of Yugoslavia's unique position.**

Yugoslavia has integrated into Western markets to the point where reorientation of her trade with the bloc nations could probably be accomplished with greater ease than could any bloc switching. This situation would place Yugoslavia in a dominant bargaining position. As early as 1905, the German economist Karl Dietzel argued that

> In respect to the question of the strength of the (bargain-
> ing) position, it does not matter so much which one of the
> two nations waging a tariff war buys more from the other;
> it matters more which of the two nations can better do
> without the market of the other, and is able in the case of
> loss of this market, to sell nearly as much elsewhere.[11]

---

*One would expect that as a country became increasingly more dependent on another, the ability to "extract gains" should increase, likely at an increasing rate.

**The original purpose of this study was only to determine the Yugoslav position. However, several possible explanations of the results suggest themselves.

The fact that Yugoslavia enjoys most-favored-nation treatment with GATT (General Agreement on Tariffs and Trade) members and has actively solicited Western contacts, would indicate that Yugoslavia should be able to buy and sell "nearly as much elsewhere."

Another cause of Yugoslavia's gain in bloc trade may be due to Western discrimination against the bloc. In our calculations we have used prices that Yugoslavia receives and pays on Western markets, the relevant Yugoslav measure. The Soviet Union and the other Comecon nations may not be able to operate on Western markets at the same terms as does Yugoslavia. This would mean that, although the Soviet Union pays Yugoslavia a higher price (higher than Yugoslavia could earn in the West) on certain items, these items would only be available to the Soviet at still higher prices on Western markets. Conversely, on imports Yugoslavia may be paying the Soviet Union a higher price than these imports could earn on Western markets. Our measure indicated that Yugoslavia was paying the Soviet Union a lower price than Yugoslavia would pay on Western markets.

A third explanation is the political situation. Political factors may place Yugoslavia in a strong bargaining position in trade matters.

SUMMARY

The purpose of this chapter has been to examine several implications of the discrimination measured in Chapter 6. It has been argued that, although quality differences enter the measure of discrimination, the evidence indicates that many of the effects of quality differences cancel out and that the observed discrimination is too great to attribute to quality difference alone. The "exchange rate effect" explanation of the observed discrimination was shown to be false. Finally, since we had argued that the discrimination was primarily a result of economic forces, a simple trade dependency hypothesis of discrimination was developed and tested. Some of the results proved statistically significant when regressions were run for each of the three years for which the level of discrimination was measured. This analysis lends support to the contention that economic forces are important in determining the terms of trade in Comecon trade. It does not suggest that political forces are unimportant.

NOTES

1. Frederic L. Pryor, The Communist Foreign Trade System (Cambridge, Mass.: The MIT Press, 1963), p. 179. Pryor is quoting Jan Wszelaki, Communist Economic Strategy: The Role of East Central Europe.

2. Irving B. Kravis and Robert E. Lipsey, The Use of Regression Methods in International Price Comparisons, Preliminary Paper, NBER (New York, 1967), pp. 3-4.

3. See Irving B. Kravis and Robert E. Lipsey, "International Price Comparisons by Regression Methods," International Economic Review, X, 2 (June 1969), 232-46. Their bibliography lists recent work in this area.

4. P. J. D. Wiles, Communist International Economics (New York: Praeger, 1969).

5. Ibid,. pp. 543, 544.

6. Alan A. Brown, "The Economics of Centrally Planned Foreign Trade: The Hungarian Experience" (unpublished Ph.D. dissertation, Harvard University, 1966), p. 224n.

7. Franklyn Holzman, "Soviet Foreign Trade Pricing and the Question of Discrimination," Review of Economics and Statistics, XLIV (May 1962), 137-47; Paul Marer, "Foreign Trade Prices in the Soviet Bloc: A Theoretical and Empirical Study" (unpublished Ph.D. dissertation, University of Pennsylvania, 1968 [University Microfilms]); Horst Mendershausen, "Terms of Trade Between the Soviet Union and Smaller Communist Countries, 1955-1957," Review of Economics and Statistics, XLI (May 1959), 106-18; Pryor, Communist Foreign Trade System; Laszlo Zsoldes, Economic Integration of Hungary into the Soviet Bloc (Columbus: The Ohio State University Press, 1963).

8. For example, see Marer, "Foreign Trade Prices," and Zsoldos, Integration of Hungary.

9. Marer, "Foreign Trade Prices," p. 224.

10. Franklyn D. Holzman, "More on Soviet Bloc Trade Discrimination," Soviet Studies, XVII (July 1965), 55.

11. Karl Dietzel, Der deutsch-amerikanische Handelsvertrag und das Phantom der amerikanischen Industriekonkurrenz (Berlin, 1905), p. 20, quoted in Albert O. Hirschman, National Power and the Structure of Foreign Trade (Berkeley: University of California Press, 1945), p. 33n.

8

It has been demonstrated that Yugoslavia occupies a unique position in world trade. A member of neither, she is associated with both the EEC and Comecon. This position might enable Yugoslavia to become a meeting place for world trade. B. Horvat has recently argued that this potential is recognized and Yugoslavia could become a center for Western, Comecon, and third-world trade.[1] This development, though possible, depends very critically on successful completion of the economic reforms to include free convertibility of the dinar. Present developments indicate this may be some time in coming. This book has attempted to answer several questions regarding Yugoslavia's foreign trade experience. We can briefly highlight some answers to these questions by summarizing the material presented in each chapter.

In Chapter 2 we found that Yugoslavia was one of the least developed countries in Europe. The trade structure of Yugoslavia after World War II was one characteristic of an underdeveloped country. In recent years, however, Yugoslavia has enjoyed one of the fastest growth rates in Europe. One result of this growth has been a change in the commodity composition and direction of her trade.

Chapter 3 demonstrated that international trade plays a more important role in Yugoslavia than in other countries of her economic class but would probably play a still larger role should she integrate more fully into either the EFTA or EEC. In this chapter we saw that Yugoslavia is relatively more involved in trade with Western markets than any of the Comecon countries. In addition Yugoslavia transacts a larger percentage of her trade with the developing countries than any of the Comecon countries.

The commodity composition of Yugoslavia's trade has changed with industrialization. The export bundle has become more industrialized, and the import bundle consists increasingly of "Goods for Reproduction."

The direction of Yugoslavia's trade has also changed in the 1960s. In the early part of the decade Yugoslavia became increasingly involved in Comecon. This participation reached a high in 1966 and has since declined. Trade with Western markets has been quite stable as a share of total trade, but there have been some marked changes in country participation. Most significantly, Yugoslav imports from the United States declined relatively throughout the decade and absolutely after 1966. Trade with the underdeveloped countries is characterized by the fact that the substantial portion of this trade is transacted with a few countries.

In Chapter 4 we briefly examined the economic reforms as they relate to international trade. The reforms have been applied to the price system, the export-import system, the tariff system, and the foreign exchange system. These reforms have been attempted in an effort to "sensitize" the Yugoslav economy to world markets. At the same time that the Yugoslav market has been consciously subjected to Western pressures, it has been insulated from Comecon pressure. A dichotomy in the institutional framework of Yugoslavia's foreign trade sector has emerged in order to deal with the state monopolies of Comecon. Chapters 5, 6, and 7 were concerned with the effects of this dual institutional framework.

After reviewing recent literature on the effects of state trading and discrimination, a model of state trading was developed and applied to the Yugoslav evidence. It was found that Yugoslavia "profits" in her trade with Comecon (when the bundle of goods was revalued at prices it would have earned and cost on Western markets). This result precipitated speculation on possible reasons for this superior bargaining position. In conclusion a model of trade dependency was formulated and tested. Some of the results were statistically significant.

LIMITATIONS OF RESULTS

This study is the first (to my knowledge) measurement of Yugoslavia's terms of trade vis-à-vis the bloc and Western countries. This application was warranted because of the institutional dichotomy which has emerged in Yugoslavia and was facilitated by the extensive data published by the Yugoslav Federal Institute for Statistics. In addition to extending the state trading literature to a new set of data, this study has utilized a larger sample than any of the previously cited studies. The results obtained are not inconsistent with other published research and are conformable to economic theory.* One caveat remains; employing such a large sample limited the analysis to a three-year period. This shortcoming prohibited the testing of any hypothesis other than our simple trade dependency hypothesis. The results obtained in Chapter 7 should, therefore, be considered preliminary. A causal explanation of Yugoslavia's discrimination requires further testing.

DIRECTION FOR FURTHER RESEARCH

Several questions left unanswered point to areas for future investigation. Among the more interesting and more difficult is the problem of quality differences. The literature cited gives no satisfactory answer to this question. Any attempt to quantify quality differences in East-West trade would be a contribution of obvious value. Of more particular relevance to this study would be its extension to cover a larger number of years. Calculating movements in the level of discrimination over a ten- to fifteen-year period might lend additional insights into the causal relationships. A heroic study calculating the level of "macro-discrimination" in each of the Comecon countries would permit a determination of the relative bargaining

---

*Western literature is replete with arguments concerning the discriminatory power of state trading monopolies. Two quotations spanning 25 years serve as evidence. "When monopoly power is present, its use tends, to some extent, to be automatic and undeliberate. The existence of the power, even without the conscious will to exploit it, is sufficient to yield some monopolistic fruits." Jacob Viner, "International Relations Between State-Controlled National Economies," American Economic Review, XXIV (March 1944), 81. "Finally, because among STE's each country is an enterprise, all trade is political: all quarrels about prices, etc., automatically rise to cabinet level if not settled lower down, involving both the state machine and national pride. Moreover, STE's are few; they would at best form an oligopoly, and in fact, choose to be a series of bilateral monopolies. Yet oligopoly is in any case, a state of economic war." P. J. D. Wiles, Communist International Economics (New York: Praeger, 1969), p. 523.

position of each country and might allow for an identification of the relevant determinants in Comecon bargaining.*

NOTE

1. Branko Horvat, "Yugoslav Economic Policy in the Post War Period: Problems, Ideas, Institutional Developments," American Economic Review, June 1971, pp. 69-169.

---

*Such a comprehensive study is, at present, infeasible because of the unavailability of data for many of the Comecon countries.

TABLE A-1

Trade Turnover Per Capita and Trade Turnover as a Percentage of GDP
in Comecon, EEC, and EFTA, 1960 and 1965*
(millions of $ U.S.: imports plus exports)

Country	GDP (millions $ U.S.) 1960	GDP (millions $ U.S.) 1965	Population (millions) 1960	Population (millions) 1965	Trade Turnover (millions $ U.S.) 1960
COMECON					
USSR	198,000	265,200	214.40	230.59	11,194
Rumania	8,900	11,800	18.40	19.03	2,214
Poland	19,100	25,800	29.70	31.42	2,821
Bulgaria	4,000	5,200	7.87	8.21	1,235
Hungary	7,200	9,500	9.98	10.15	1,850
E. Germany	18,200	21,700	17.24	17.01	3,947
Czechoslovakia	16,400	18,400	13.65	14.16	3,746
Albania	250	345	1.61	1.86	130
EEC					
Italy	33,590	56,742	49.64	51.58	8,373
France	60,380	94,044	45.68	48.92	13,138
W. Germany	74,184	116,713	55.43	59.04	21,519
Netherlands	11,236	18,829	11.48	12.29	8,559
Belgium	11,320	16,660	9.15	9.46	
Luxembourg	494	632	0.31	0.33	7,760
EFTA					
Portugal	2,519	3,689	8.83	9.23	874
Austria	6,182	9,341	7.05	7.26	2,536
UK	70,840	97,720	52.36	54.59	22,853
Norway	4,578	7,093	3.60	3.72	2,344
Sweden	12,294	19,223	7.48	7.73	5,463
Denmark	5,951	10,040	4.43	4.76	3,299
Switzerland	8,491	13,688	5.36	5.95	4,123
Other					
Yugoslavia	4,315	7,240	18.40	19.51	1,392
Greece	3,412	5,751	8.83	8.54	905
Spain	10,266	21,420	30.30	31.42	1,447
Brazil	17,179	22,173	70.97	81.30	2,731
Colombia	4,551	5,427	15.42	17.79	984
India	33,342	49,623	429.03	486.81	3,658
Indonesia	6,016	7,371	94.20	105.30	1,419
Pakistan	7,287	10,028	94.65	102.88	1,087
Turkey	5,694	8,745	27.75	31.39	789
Ghana	1,342	2,232	6.78	7.74	657
Tunisia	798	960	4.23	4.68	309
Libya	171	1,142	1.30	1.62	180
UAR	3,905	4,701	25.83	29.60	1,235

(continued)

129

TABLE A-1 (Continued)

Trade Turnover (millions $ U.S.) 1965	Trade Per Capita ($ 1960)	Trade Per Capita ($ 1965)	Trade/GDP 1960	Trade/GDP 1965	Change in Trade per Capita & Trade per GDP (1960 = 100)	
16,233	75.7	70.4	.05	.06	92	120
3,442	120.2	180.9	.24	.29	150	120
4,568	94.9	145.4	.14	.17	153	121
2,354	156.9	286.7	.30	.45	182	150
3,031	185.4	290.6	.25	.31	161	124
5,322	228.9	312.8	.21	.24	136	114
5,362	274.4	378.7	.22	.29	138	131
158	80.7	84.9	.52	.45	105	86
14,578	168.7	282.6	.24	.25	168	104
20,390	287.6	416.8	.21	.21	145	100
35,364	388.2	599.0	.29	.30	154	103
13,854	745.6	1,127.3	.76	.73	151	96
12,896	820.3	1,317.3	.65	.74	161	113
1,500	99.0	162.5	.34	.40	164	117
3,701	359.7	509.8	.41	.39	142	95
28,857	436.5	528.6	.32	.29	121	90
3,653	651.1	982.0	.51	.51	151	100
8,344	730.3	706.8	.44	.43	97	97
5,143	744.7	1,080.5	.51	.51	145	100
6,656	769.2	1,118.7	.48	.48	145	100
2,380	75.7	122.0	.32	.32	161	100
1,462	108.6	171.2	.26	.25	158	96
3,971	47.7	126.4	.14	.18	265	128
2,692	38.5	33.1	.15	.12	86	80
993	63.8	55.8	.21	.18	87	85
4,613	8.5	7.5	.10	.09	112	90
1,426	15.1	13.5	.23	.19	89	82
1,571	11.1	15.3	.14	.15	138	107
988	28.4	31.5	.13	.11	111	84
736	96.9	95.1	.48	.32	98	66
365	73.1	78.0	.38	.38	107	100
1,117	138.5	690.0	1.05	1.05	498	100
1,537	47.8	51.9	.32	.32	109	103

*Albania was a member of Comecon from 1949-62. Trade turnover figures for the year 1963 are used instead of 1965.

Source: GDP and population figures from E. Hagen and O. Hawrylyshyn, "Analysis of World Income and Growth, 1955-1965," Economic Development and Cultural Change, XVIII, Part II, October 1969. Trade turnover data from United Nations, Yearbook of International Trade Statistics (New York: United Nations, 1967), pp. 14, 15.

TABLE A-2

Exports by Branch of Economic Activity, 1960-69*

Branch	1960 %	1961 %	1962 %	1963 %	1964 Quantity	1964 Value
Industry	74.8	74.7	79.0	76.6	5,020,585	8,750,996
Electric energy in MWH	0.2	0.1	0.2	0.3	38,963	3,937
Coal and coal derivatives	0.4	0.4	0.2	0.2	167,216	16,818
Crude petroleum and derivatives	0.6	1.0	2.2	1.5	482,050	134,556
Iron and steel metallurgy	3.7	3.6	4.0	2.7	370,056	267,304
Nonferrous metallurgy	10.0	9.1	9.1	8.5	1,607,875	1,035,915
Nonmetals	2.6	2.5	2.8	2.5	608,711	343,490
Metal industry	12.0	11.9	13.2	11.2	176,579	1,325,499
Shipbuilding	3.3	4.9	9.5	7.0	76,623	509,403
Electrical energy	4.3	4.6	4.2	4.7	56,362	479,916
Chemical industry	2.9	2.6	2.4	2.7	276,991	414,197
Building material industry	0.2	0.2	0.2	0.2	62,121	21,682
Timber industry	12.1	11.5	11.1	11.0	810,451	1,189,763
Paper industry	1.4	1.1	1.3	1.7	86,251	187,950
Textile industry	5.9	6.4	6.0	7.7	49,961	991,547
Leather and footwear industry	2.4	2.4	2.5	3.6	10,015	505,811
Rubber industry	0.0	0.1	0.1	0.1	2,643	28,232
Foodstuffs industry	9.2	9.4	7.0	7.2	154,197	806,181
Printing industry	0.0	0.1	0.0	0.1	603	15,403
Tobacco industry	3.5	2.7	3.0	3.7	21,876	471,223
Film industry	0.1	0.1	0.0	0.0	4	2,139
Agriculture	23.2	22.9	19.0	21.1	407,554	2,185,655
Agriculture	8.9	6.2	2.5	3.3	79,694	286,872
Fruits	0.5	0.6	1.2	0.7	61,469	103,566
Livestock	10.7	13.4	12.2	14.0	165,161	1,504,074
Fisheries	0.3	0.3	0.3	0.2	3,532	23,268
Home-processed agricultural prod.	2.8	2.4	2.8	2.9	97,698	267,875
Forestry	2.0	2.4	2.0	2.3	837,502	227,781
Forest exploitation	1.3	1.6	1.0	1.4	826,842	143,487
Hunting and medicinal herbs	0.7	0.8	1.0	0.9	10,660	84,224
Total	100.0	100.0	100.0	100.0	6,265,641	11,164,402

(continued)

131

Branch	%	Quantity	1965 Value	%	Quantity	1966 Value	%
Industry	78.3	5,032,119	11,075,142	81.2	6,267,839	12,424,548	81.5
Electric							
energy in MWH	0.0	48,822	3,408	0.0	20,694	2,256	0.0
Coal and coal							
derivatives	0.2	131,062	11,860	0.1	117,464	11,202	0.1
Crude petroleum							
and derivatives	1.2	423,536	121,721	0.9	1,170,196	252,664	1.7
Iron and steel							
metallurgy	2.4	250,600	265,740	1.9	183,213	297,949	1.9
Nonferrous							
metallurgy	9.3	1,530,351	1,282,464	9.4	1,875,932	1,482,944	9.7
Nonmetals	3.1	624,092	406,236	3.0	538,043	392,265	2.6
Metal industry	11.9	268,602	2,049,491	15.0	277,451	2,341,682	15.4
Shipbuilding	4.6	124,103	988,369	7.2	156,236	1,103,428	7.2
Electrical energy	4.3	69,715	770,964	5.7	70,810	951,777	6.3
Chemical industry	3.7	489,242	681,877	5.0	605,515	794,599	5.2
Building material							
industry	0.2	54,347	21,037	0.2	52,637	20,604	0.2
Timber industry	10.6	743,014	1,199,822	8.8	795,577	1,274,220	8.3
Paper industry	1.6	99,665	234,691	1.7	133,920	220,748	1.9
Textile industry	8.9	53,015	1,146,188	8.4	56,760	1,328,435	8.7
Leather and							
footwear industry	4.5	9,753	535,635	3.9	14,071	614,624	4.0
Rubber industry	0.3	4,030	36,734	0.3	5,406	57,471	0.4
Foodstuffs industry	7.2	134,085	857,938	6.3	193,037	774,165	5.1
Printing industry	0.1	755	22,532	0.2	1,100	21,256	0.1
Tobacco industry	4.2	22,146	435,947	3.2	20,466	410,110	2.7
Film industry	0.0	6	2,488	0.0	5	2,149	0.0
Agriculture	19.6	439,971	2,362,714	17.3	781,774	2,654,374	17.4
Agriculture	2.6	142,208	349,051	2.6	503,902	602,908	4.0
Fruits	0.9	35,309	60,236	0.4	19,684	41,872	0.3
Livestock	13.5	167,248	1,651,027	12.1	176,073	1,729,534	11.3
Fisheries	0.2	2,303	16,667	0.1	2,344	16,687	0.1
Home-processed							
agricultural prod.	2.4	92,903	285,733	2.1	79,781	263,373	1.7
Forestry	2.1	655,743	205,984	1.5	468,271	172,080	1.1
Forest emploitation	1.3	644,057	124,272	0.9	457,491	85,783	0.5
Hunting and medicinal							
herbs	0.8	11,686	81,712	0.6	10,780	86,297	0.6
Total	100.0	6,127,833	13,643,840	100.0	7,517,884	15,251,002	100.0

132

Branch	Quantity	1967 Value	%	Quantity	1968 Value	%	Quantity	1969 Value	%
Industry	6,624,298	12,386,463	79.2	6,319,111	13,150,751	83.3	6,738,192	15,551,745	84.4
Electric energy in MWH	174,334	18,466	0.1	42,004	4,227	0.0	55,968	2,876	0.0
Coal and coal derivatives	144,045	15,069	0.1	105,696	10,448	0.1	231,760	59,609	0.3
Crude petroleum and derivatives	1,030,248	248,721	1.6	572,848	143,461	0.9	459,519	129,386	0.8
Iron and steel metallurgy	429,419	396,733	2.5	373,571	360,681	2.3	427,174	438,657	2.4
Nonferrous metallurgy	2,105,601	1,353,388	8.7	2,262,311	1,845,953	11.8	2,476,506	2,543,321	13.8
Nonmetals	519,395	374,903	2.4	531,378	405,052	2.6	608,495	475,071	2.6
Metal industry	226,518	2,071,955	13.3	213,497	1,937,265	12.3	210,460	2,050,205	11.2
Shipbuilding	116,102	734,777	4.7	143,327	1,024,101	6.5	178,081	1,258,747	6.8
Electrical energy	69,683	995,792	6.4	69,236	1,058,745	6.7	75,151	1,224,892	6.6
Chemical industry	514,396	859,951	5.5	601,210	887,651	5.6	394,379	1,070,722	5.8
Building material industry	237,898	40,966	0.3	95,734	26,616	0.2	103,679	25,592	0.2
Timber industry	767,776	1,225,883	7.8	823,271	1,362,415	8.6	942,101	1,568,791	8.5
Paper industry	143,268	316,874	2.0	203,131	423,377	2.7	202,835	445,187	2.4
Textile industry	57,297	1,526,980	9.8	74,778	1,646,289	10.4	88,731	2,017,950	10.9
Leather and footwear industry	22,705	858,422	5.5	19,318	891,844	5.6	18,256	938,415	5.1
Rubber industry	4,808	50,046	0.3	6,307	53,630	0.3	6,655	67,760	0.4
Foodstuffs industry	214,906	899,258	5.7	206,252	715,142	4.5	298,896	927,596	5.0
Printing industry	1,368	22,500	0.1	1,739	33,372	0.2	2,195	43,230	0.2
Tobacco industry	18,860	373,065	2.4	15,500	316,521	2.0	13,314	259,721	1.4
Film industry	5	2,714	0.0	7	3,961	0.0	5	4,017	0.0
Agriculture	1,273,570	3,095,265	19.8	797,699	2,451,135	15.5	775,150	2,648,060	14.4
Agriculture	961,417	910,872	5.8	502,297	594,718	3.8	427,937	512,123	2.8
Fruits	29,568	53,335	0.2	14,727	34,964	0.2	44,926	86,140	0.5
Livestock	191,935	1,843,672	11.8	197,375	1,543,878	9.8	199,287	1,724,186	9.4
Fisheries	2,788	18,426	0.1	2,372	17,479	0.1	1,986	16,027	0.1
Home-processed agricultural prod.	87,862	268,960	1.7	80,928	260,096	1.6	101,014	309,584	1.6
Forestry	418,501	164,075	1.0	492,610	194,392	1.2	640,339	231,194	1.2
Forest exploitation	403,580	76,861	0.5	478,610	92,914	0.6	630,459	128,258	0.7
Hunting and medicinal herbs	14,921	87,214	0.5	14,000	101,478	0.6	9,880	102,936	0.5
Total	8,316,369	15,645,803	100.0	7,609,420	15,796,278	100.0	8,153,681	18,430,999	100.0

*Quantity in million tons, value in thousands of new dinars (12.5 new dinars = $1). Quantity and value for 1960-63 not reproduced.

Source: Statistika Spoljne Trgovine SFR Jugoslavije (Belgrade: Federal Institute for Statistics), 1961, p. 26; 1964, p. 27; 1966, p. 29; 1961, p. 31.

133

TABLE A-3

Imports by Use of Product, 1960-69*

Use	1960	1961	1962	1963	1964 Value	%	1965 Value
	%						
Reproduction goods	56.8	52.3	54.3	57.7	10,342,137	62.5	9,997,849
Crude materials and semi-products	35.5	33.4	35.4	38.7	6,899,233	41.7	6,755,648
Mineral fuels	5.5	4.4	5.4	4.5	824,757	5.0	899,540
Manufactured goods for reproduction	15.8	14.5	13.5	14.5	2,618,197	15.8	2,342,661
Investment goods and equipment	28.5	28.2	25.2	20.0	3,564,569	21.6	3,174,832
Power-generating machinery	2.8	2.2	1.5	0.7	120,659	0.7	81,475
Agricultural machinery	2.9	0.3	0.3	0.4	115,504	0.7	92,040
Metal-working machinery	1.5	1.8	4.1	2.7	686,992	4.2	495,620
Other machinery	11.9	13.1	12.8	10.1	1,532,305	9.3	1,394,683
Electric motors and other equipment	2.8	2.8	2.6	2.9	369,835	2.2	319,026
Transport equipment	5.2	6.5	2.6	1.9	424,636	2.6	565,484
Other investment goods	1.4	1.5	1.3	1.3	314,638	1.9	226,504
Consumer goods	14.7	19.5	20.5	22.3	2,632,928	15.9	2,926,711
Food	8.1	12.6	14.0	16.1	1,614,606	9.8	1,939,625
Beverages and tobacco	0.0	0.1	0.4	0.7	31,655	0.2	6,810
Clothing and footwear	0.4	0.5	0.5	0.4	76,145	0.4	67,724
Furniture	0.0	0.0	0.0	0.0	4,536	0.0	4,485
Textile articles excl. footwear	1.8	2.2	2.1	1.5	311,787	1.9	335,647
Medicinal, pharmaceutical and cosmetic products	1.0	1.0	1.0	0.9	128,068	0.8	125,732
Other consumer goods	3.4	3.1	2.5	2.7	466,130	2.8	446,686
Total	100.0	100.0	100.0	100.0	16,539,694	100.0	16,099,392

	1965 %	1966 Value	%	1967 Value	%	1968 Value	%	1969 Value	%
	62.1	11,333,904	57.5	12,214,593	57.2	12,770,151	56.9	16,057,251	63.2
	42.0	7,488,223	38.0	7,838,805	36.7	7,994,710	35.6	10,311,498	38.7
	5.6	1,030,233	5.2	1,056,956	5.0	1,224,422	5.5	1,293,981	4.8
	14.5	2,815,448	14.3	3,318,832	15.5	3,551,019	15.8	4,451,772	16.7
	19.7	4,281,757	21.8	4,633,481	21.7	5,593,280	24.9	5,941,360	22.3
	0.5	236,725	1.2	73,326	0.3	244,734	1.1	188,079	0.7
	0.6	195,268	1.0	269,404	1.3	239,889	1.1	232,442	0.9
	3.1	541,033	2.7	419,145	2.0	304,440	1.4	384,326	1.4
	8.6	1,573,547	8.0	1,975,985	9.2	2,560,462	11.4	2,732,326	10.3
	2.0	428,811	2.2	453,168	2.1	555,911	2.5	720,547	2.7
	3.5	939,137	4.8	931,325	4.4	1,018,231	4.5	968,539	3.6
	1.4	367,236	1.9	511,128	2.4	669,613	2.9	715,103	2.7
	18.2	4,077,218	20.7	4,493,570	21.1	4,096,814	18.2	4,673,560	17.5
	12.1	2,511,569	12.8	1,887,660	8.9	1,057,571	4.7	1,187,158	4.5
	0.0	74,017	0.4	94,199	0.4	46,544	0.2	75,423	0.3
	0.4	81,987	0.4	193,952	0.9	310,117	1.4	350,785	1.3
	0.0	6,084	0.0	2,916	0.0	6,693	0.0	13,749	0.1
	2.1	562,330	2.8	588,528	2.8	726,773	3.2	757,144	2.8
	0.8	155,226	0.8	132,290	0.6	160,076	0.7	199,046	0.7
	2.8	686,005	3.5	1,594,025	7.5	1,789,040	8.0	2,090,255	7.8
Total	100.0	19,692,879	100.0	21,341,644	100.0	22,460,245	100.0	26,672,171	100.0

*Value in thousands of new dinars (12.5 new dinars= $1). The quantity and value for 1960-63 were not reproduced.

Source: Statistika Spoljne Trgovine SFR Jugoslavije (Belgrade: Federal Institute for Statistics), 1964, p. 28; 1966, p. 30; 1960, p. 30.

TABLE A-4

Exports and Imports by Stage of Production, 1960–69*
(value in thousand new dinars)

Stage of Production	1960 %	1961 %	1962 %	1963 %	Quantity	1964 Value	%	Quantity	1965 Value	%	Quantity	1966 Value	%
Exports													
Crude articles	25.7	24.7	19.6	20.8	3,301,944	1,908,648	17.1	2,604,033	1,711,680	12.5	3,175,016	2,050,246	13.4
Simply transformed articles	38.7	38.4	37.6	36.7	2,115,641	4,302,214	38.5	2,437,544	4,566,329	33.5	3,243,827	5,063,993	33.2
More elaborately transformed articles	35.6	36.9	42.8	42.5	848,056	4,953,540	44.4	1,086,256	7,365,831	54.0	1,099,041	8,136,763	53.4
Total	100.0	100.0	100.0	100.0	6,265,641	11,164,402	100.0	6,127,833	13,643,840	100.0	7,517,884	15,251,002	100.0
EXPORTS													
Crude articles	20.2	24.2	26.6	30.4	4,632,461	3,903,323	23.6	5,618,874	4,517,356	28.1	6,742,469	4,858,999	24.7
Simply transformed articles	22.7	21.6	22.1	21.8	4,390,459	4,073,804	24.6	3,618,394	3,741,042	23.2	4,381,878	4,475,189	22.7
More elaborately transformed articles	57.1	54.2	51.3	47.8	860,897	8,562,567	51.8	744,929	7,840,994	48.7	1,130,392	10,358,690	52.6
Total	100.0	100.0	100.0	100.0	9,883,817	16,539,694	100.0	9,982,197	16,099,392	100.0	12,254,739	19,692,879	100.0

Stage of Production	1967			1968			1969		
	Quantity	Value	%	Quantity	Value	%	Quantity	Value	%
Exports									
Crude articles	8,036,843	2,489,650	15.9	3,704,304	2,220,840	14.1	4,000,521	2,304,727	12.5
Simply transformed articles	3,048,236	4,925,751	31.5	2,771,768	5,053,435	32.0	2,815,333	6,296,161	34.2
More elaborately transformed articles	1,231,290	8,230,402	52.6	1,133,348	8,522,003	53.9	1,337,827	9,830,111	53.3
Total	8,316,369	15,645,803	100.0	7,609,420	15,796,278	100.0	8,153,681	18,430,999	100.0
Imports									
Crude articles	5,554,896	3,779,721	17.7	5,891,688	3,474,286	15.5	6,923,758	4,473,844	16.8
Simply transformed articles	5,333,305	5,324,892	25.0	5,287,720	5,149,173	22.9	5,514,017	6,160,695	23.1
More elaborately transformed articles	1,148,771	12,237,031	57.3	1,098,184	13,856,786	61.6	1,309,891	16,037,632	60.1
Total	12,036,972	21,341,644	100.0	12,277,592	22,460,245	100.0	13,747,666	26,672,171	100.0

*The quantity and value for 1960–63 are not reported here.

Source: Statistika Spoljne Trgovine SFR Jugoslavije, (Belgrade: Federal Institute for Statistics), 1960, p. 25; 1964, p. 26; 1966, p. 28; 1969, p. 30.

TABLE A-5

Exports by Country, 1950, 1955, 1960-69*

(country of payment)

Country	1950 Value	1950 % of Total	1950 % of Group	1955 Value	1955 % of Total	1955 % of Group	1960 Value	1960 % of Total	1960 % of Group	1961 Value	1961 % of Total
1 Albania				58	0.1	0.6	95	0.0	0.2	51	0.0
2 Bulgaria				164	0.2	1.6	2,749	1.6	5.1	2,382	1.4
3 Czechoslovakia				2,105	2.8	20.1	7,640	4.6	14.1	5,068	3.0
4 E. Germany				556	0.7	5.3	13,464	7.9	24.8	8,080	4.7
5 Hungary				780	1.0	7.5	6,051	3.6	11.1	5,339	3.1
6 Poland				1,156	1.5	11.0	6,593	3.9	12.1	12,142	7.1
7 Rumania				254	0.3	2.4	1,306	0.8	2.4	3,127	1.8
8 USSR				5,385	7.0	51.5	16,452	9.7	30.2	16,147	9.5
9 Total Comecon				10,458	13.6	100.0	54,350	32.0	100.0	52,336	30.7
10 Belgium-Luxembourg	2,412	3.0	3.6	785	1.0	1.5	1,403	0.8	1.7	2,364	0.8
11 France	2,752	3.5	4.1	2,727	3.6	5.4	2,612	1.5	3.2	2,911	1.7
12 Netherlands	3,050	3.9	4.6	1,963	2.6	3.9	1,804	1.1	2.2	1,701	1.0
13 Italy	9,296	11.7	13.9	11,789	15.3	23.2	22,375	13.2	27.8	21,042	12.3
14 W. Germany	9,857	12.4	14.7	9,776	12.7	19.3	14,531	8.6	18.1	16,614	9.7
15 Total EEC	27,367	34.5	40.9	27,040	35.1	53.3	42,725	25.2	53.1	43,632	25.6
16 Austria	8,484	10.7	12.7	4,576	6.0	9.0	9,136	5.4	11.4	7,992	4.7
17 Denmark	466	0.6	0.7	258	0.3	0.5	455	0.3	0.6	560	0.3
18 Portugal											
19 Sweden	1,942	2.5	2.9	418	0.6	0.8	1,485	0.8	1.8	1,701	1.0
20 Switzerland	3,153	4.0	4.7	4,016	5.2	7.9	2,555	1.5	3.2	2,347	1.4
21 UK	14,785	18.6	22.8	6,337	8.2	12.5	14,288	8.4	17.8	14,449	8.5
22 Total EFTA	28,830	36.4	43.0	15,605	20.3	30.7	27,919	16.4	34.7	27,058	15.9
23 United States	10,716	13.5	16.0	8,134	10.6	16.0	9,744	5.7	12.1	11,779	6.9
24 Total EEC, EFTA, and U.S.	66,913	84.4	100.0	50,779	66.0	100.0	80,388	47.3	100.0	82,469	48.3
25 Algeria	32	0.0	0.3	339	0.4	2.4	331	0.2	1.1	149	0.1
26 Ethiopia				74	0.1	0.5	487	0.3	1.7	151	0.1
27 Ghana							69	0.0	0.2	218	0.1
28 Guinea										490	0.3
29 Ivory Coast										24	0.0
30 Kenya											
31 Mali											
32 Morocco	248	0.3	2.6	341	0.5	2.4	121	0.0	0.4	182	0.1
33 Sudan				13	0.0	0.1	316	0.2	1.1	504	0.3
34 Liberia							1	0.0	0.0	10	0.0
35 Tunisia	10	0.0	0.1	68	0.1	0.5	656	0.5	2.2	434	0.3

Country	1950 Value	1950 % of Total	1950 % of Group	1955 Value	1955 % of Total	1955 % of Group	1960 Value	1960 % of Total	1960 % of Group	1961 Value	1961 % of Total
36 Uganda							39	0.0	0.1		
37 Total Africa	290	0.3	3.1	835	1.1	3.9	2,020	1.2	6.9	2,162	1.3
38 Burma				12	0.0	0.1	1,317	0.8	4.5	576	0.4
39 Cambodia							73	0.0	0.2	362	0.2
40 Ceylon				19	0.0	0.1	27	0.0	0.1	49	0.0
41 India	93	0.1	1.0	72	0.1	0.5	2,263	1.3	7.7	4,937	2.9
42 Indonesia				115	0.2	0.8	3,555	2.2	12.2	4,600	2.7
43 Malaysia										8	0.0
44 Pakistan							596	0.4	2.0	462	0.3
45 Thailand				30	0.0	0.2	2	0.0	0.0	762	0.5
46 Total Asia	93	0.1	1.0	248	0.3	1.7	7,832	4.6	26.8	11,756	6.8
47 Spain							396	0.2	1.4	624	0.4
48 Total Europe							396	0.2	1.4	624	0.4
49 Argentina	4,066	5.1	42.8	819	1.1	5.8	592	0.4	2.0	1,276	0.7
50 Brazil	541	0.7	5.7	4,048	5.3	28.4	1,713	1.1	5.9	604	0.4
51 Cuba				32	0.0	0.2	130	0.0	0.4	1,411	0.8
52 Chile							168	0.0	0.6	89	0.1
53 Colombia							10	0.0	0.0	31	0.0
54 Mexico	2	0.0	0.0	20	0.0	0.1	232	0.1	0.8	8	0.0
55 Peru	116	0.2	1.2				14	0.0	0.0	127	0.1
56 Uruguay	3	0.0	0.0	15	0.0	0.1				15	0.0
57 Venezuela							2,859	1.7	9.8	3,552	2.1
58 Total Latin and S. America	4,728	6.0	49.8	4,934	6.4	34.7	4,920	2.9	16.8	5,884	3.5
59 Cyprus	57	0.1	0.6	163	0.2	1.1	184	0.1	0.6	367	0.2
60 Greece	77	0.1	0.8	1,627	2.1	11.4	588	0.3	2.0	242	0.2
61 Iran				19	0.0	0.1	468	0.2	1.6	389	0.2
62 Iraq				118	0.2	0.8	1,321	0.8	4.5		
63 Israel	593	0.8	6.2	1,186	1.5	8.3	1,246	0.8	4.3	2,278	1.3
64 Jordan				164	0.2	1.2	179	0.0	0.6	90	0.1
65 Lebanon	35	0.0	0.4	910	1.2	6.4	626	0.5	2.1	312	0.2
66 Libya				59	0.1	0.4				317	0.2
67 Turkey	325	0.4	3.4	3,303	4.3	23.2	929	0.6	3.2	762	0.5
68 UAR	3,300	4.1	34.7	665	0.9	4.7	5,736	3.4	19.6	5,030	3.0
69 Total Middle East	4,387	5.5	46.1	8,214	10.7	57.7	16,147	9.5	55.2	15,671	9.2
70 Total Underdeveloped	9,498	12.0	100.0	14,231	18.5	100.0	29,254	17.2	100.0	33,765	19.8

(Continued)

139

TABLE A-5 (continued)

	1961 % of Group	1962 Value	1962 % of Total	1962 % of Group	1963 Value	1963 % of Total	1963 % of Group	1964 Value	1964 % of Total	1964 % of Group	1965 Value	1965 % of Total	1965 % of Group
1	0.1	157	0.1	0.3	91	0.0	0.1	10,657	0.1	0.3	22,702	0.2	0.4
2	4.6	1,717	0.8	3.4	2,667	1.0	4.2	123,473	1.1	3.2	217,018	1.6	3.8
3	9.7	6,335	3.1	12.7	6,958	2.9	11.0	560,209	5.0	14.5	887,796	6.5	15.6
4	15.4	10,214	4.9	20.5	11,286	4.8	17.8	790,609	7.1	20.5	949,729	7.0	16.6
5	10.2	3,285	1.6	6.6	3,647	1.6	5.8	298,513	2.7	7.7	323,327	2.4	5.7
6	23.2	12,689	6.1	25.5	11,466	4.8	18.1	495,392	4.4	12.8	803,345	5.9	14.1
7	6.0	2,127	1.0	4.3	1,477	0.6	2.3	122,518	1.1	3.2	160,431	1.2	2.8
8	30.9	13,281	6.4	26.7	25,697	10.9	40.6	1,455,577	13.0	37.7	2,343,762	17.2	41.1
9	100.0	49,805	24.0	100.0	63,289	26.7	100.0	3,856,948	34.5	100.0	5,708,110	41.8	100.0
10	1.7	1,382	0.7	1.3	1,234	0.5	1.0	71,066	0.6	1.4	89,480	0.6	1.6
11	3.5	2,932	1.4	2.8	5,297	2.2	4.1	236,958	2.1	4.5	222,358	1.6	4.0
12	2.1	1,641	0.8	1.6	2,038	0.9	1.6	118,313	1.1	2.3	131,031	0.9	2.4
13	25.5	28,532	13.8	27.2	47,248	19.9	36.6	1,649,112	14.8	31.5	1,824,027	13.4	32.7
14	20.1	20,320	9.8	19.3	22,973	9.7	17.8	962,865	8.6	18.3	1,158,390	8.5	20.8
15	52.9	54,807	26.5	52.3	78,790	33.2	61.0	3,038,314	27.2	58.0	3,425,286	25.1	61.4
16	9.7	8,483	4.1	8.1	8,623	3.6	6.7	383,876	3.4	7.3	325,758	2.4	5.8
17	0.7	671	0.3	0.6	1,002	0.4	0.8	63,662	0.6	1.2	48,437	0.3	0.9
18													
19	2.1	1,884	0.9	1.8	3,570	1.5	2.7	99,220	0.9	1.9	109,167	0.8	2.0
20	2.8	5,994	2.9	5.7	4,665	2.0	3.6	229,461	2.1	4.4	268,746	2.0	4.8
21	17.5	14,918	7.2	14.2	17,078	7.2	13.2	740,932	6.6	14.1	557,184	4.1	9.9
22	37.8	31,950	15.4	30.5	34,938	14.7	27.1	1,517,151	13.6	28.9	1,309,292	9.6	23.4
23	14.3	17,958	8.7	17.1	15,336	6.5	11.9	686,257	6.2	13.1	839,589	6.1	15.1
24	100.0	104,715	50.6	100.0	129,064	54.4	100.0	5,241,722	47.0	100.0	5,574,167	40.9	100.0
25	0.4	715	0.4	1.4	892	0.4	2.1	63,143	0.6	3.2	44,244	0.3	2.0
26	0.4	287	0.1	0.6	828	0.4	1.9	18,047	0.2	0.9	23,115	0.2	1.0
27	0.6	1,004	0.5	2.0	639	0.3	1.5	31,847	0.3	1.6	155,462	1.2	6.9
28	1.5	1,010	0.5	2.0	528	0.2	1.2	4,830	0.0	0.2	17,325	0.1	0.8
29	0.1				27	0.0	0.1	2,018	0.0	0.1	8,812	0.1	0.4
30								756	0.0	0.0	2,955	0.0	0.1
31	0.5	46	0.0	0.1	275	0.1	0.6	2,088	0.0	0.1	15,878	0.1	0.7
32	1.5	623	0.3	1.2	730	0.3	1.7	14,108	0.1	0.7	10,074	0.1	0.4
33	0.0	1,354	0.7	2.7	587	0.3	1.4	51,894	0.5	2.7	33,120	0.2	1.5
34	1.3	1,245	0.6	2.4	3,826	1.6	9.0	43,510	0.4	2.3	1,106	0.0	0.0
35		681	0.3	1.3	1,015	0.4	2.4	44,315	0.4	2.3	39,792	0.3	1.8

	1961 % of Group	1962 Value	1962 % of Total	1962 % of Group	1963 Value	1963 % of Total	1963 % of Group	1964 Value	1964 % of Total	1964 % of Group	1965 Value	1965 % of Total	1965 % of Group
36	6.4	6,965	3.7	13.7	9,347	3.9	21.9	245	0.0	0.0	434	0.0	0.0
37	1.7	399	0.2	0.8	431	0.2	1.0	276,801	2.5	14.3	352,316	2.6	15.6
38	1.1	148	0.1	0.3	233	0.1	0.5	22,119	0.2	1.1	55,976	0.4	2.5
39	0.1	20	0.0	0.0	147	0.1	0.3	3,633	0.0	0.2	36,020	0.3	1.6
40	14.6	5,574	2.7	10.9	4,494	1.9	10.5	8,830	0.1	0.5	3,761	0.0	0.2
41	13.6	10,914	5.2	21.4	6,623	2.8	15.5	352,417	3.2	18.3	370,811	2.7	16.6
42	0.0	16	0.0	0.0	24	0.0	0.1	227,175	2.0	11.8	321,519	2.5	14.4
43	1.4	412	0.2	0.5	459	0.2	1.1	692	0.0	0.0	6,405	0.0	0.3
44	2.3	1,179	0.6	2.3	1,332	0.6	3.1	93,446	0.8	4.8	90,303	0.7	4.1
45	34.8	18,662	9.0	36.6	13,743	5.8	32.2	7,310	0.1	0.4	1,264	0.0	0.1
46	1.8	425	0.2	0.8	390	0.2	0.9	715,622	6.4	37.1	886,059	6.5	39.8
47	1.8	425	0.2	0.8	390	0.2	0.9	31,470	0.3	1.6	26,061	0.2	1.2
48	3.8	4,814	2.4	9.4	1,238	0.5	2.9	31,470	0.3	1.6	26,061	0.2	1.2
49	1.8	4,047	2.0	7.9	2,190	0.9	5.1	2,806	0.0	0.1	1,803	0.0	0.1
50	4.2	143	0.1	0.3	935	0.4	2.1	191,516	1.7	9.9	31,773	0.3	1.4
51					15	0.0	0.0	40,973	0.4	2.1	61,822	0.5	2.7
52					221	0.1	0.5	9,966	0.1	0.5	1,247	0.0	0.1
53	0.3	44	0.0	0.1	19	0.0	0.0	18,213	0.2	0.9	16,570	0.1	0.7
54	0.1	17	0.0	0.0	150	0.1	0.4	564	0.0	0.0	1,303	0.0	0.1
55	0.0	8	0.0	0.0	33	0.0	0.1	774	0.0	0.0	2,845	0.0	0.1
56	0.4	235	0.1	0.5				1,341	0.0	0.1	562	0.0	0.0
57	0.0	14	0.0	0.0				1,499	0.0	0.1	1,845	0.0	0.0
58	10.5	9,322	4.5	18.3	4,801	2.0	11.2	267,652	2.4	13.9	119,770	0.8	5.4
59	1.1	289	0.1	0.6	378	0.2	0.9	11,541	0.1	0.6	16,620	0.1	0.7
60	17.4	3,107	1.5	6.1	2,795	1.2	6.6	195,728	1.8	10.1	277,738	2.0	12.4
61	0.7	341	0.2	0.7	312	0.1	0.7	32,112	0.3	1.7	78,114	0.6	3.5
62	1.2	684	0.3	1.3	543	0.2	1.3	34,931	0.3	1.8	34,625	0.3	1.5
63	6.7	2,630	1.3	5.2	2,173	0.9	5.1	102,423	0.9	5.3	70,404	0.5	3.2
64	0.3	113	0.0	0.2	305	0.1	0.7	14,028	0.1	0.7	13,791	0.1	0.6
65	0.9	414	0.2	0.8	627	0.3	1.5	21,225	0.2	1.1	29,787	0.2	1.3
66	0.9	464	0.2	0.9	479	0.2	1.2	16,195	0.1	0.8	19,022	0.1	0.9
67	2.3	1,179	0.6	2.3	1,332	0.6	3.1	51,535	0.5	2.7	49,528	0.4	2.2
68	14.9	6,381	3.1	12.5	5,447	2.3	12.8	159,105	1.5	8.2	254,814	2.0	11.4
69	46.4	15,602	7.5	30.6	14,391	6.1	33.7	638,823	5.7	33.1	844,443	6.2	37.9
70	100.0	50,976	24.6	100.0	42,672	18.0	100.0	1,930,368	17.3	100.0	2,228,649	16.3	100.0

(continued)

TABLE A-5 (Continued)

	1966 Value	1966 % of Total	1966 % of Group	1967 Value	1967 % of Total	1967 % of Group	1968 Value	1968 % of Total	1968 % of Group	1969 Value	1969 % of Total	1969 % of Group
1	24,566	0.2	0.4	34,378	0.2	0.6	17,956	0.1	0.3	37,736	0.2	0.7
2	159,729	1.0	2.9	205,008	1.3	3.7	324,990	2.1	6.2	225,049	1.2	4.2
3	844,670	5.5	15.3	624,212	4.0	11.2	678,203	4.3	13.0	777,227	4.2	14.5
4	802,671	5.3	14.5	781,503	5.0	14.1	665,633	4.2	12.8	509,834	2.8	9.5
5	365,803	2.4	6.6	336,026	2.4	6.1	355,900	2.3	6.8	542,622	2.9	10.1
6	703,851	4.6	12.7	572,363	3.6	10.3	461,964	2.9	8.7	585,785	3.2	10.9
7	208,703	1.4	3.8	279,469	1.8	5.0	262,284	1.7	5.0	265,039	1.4	4.9
8	2,421,848	15.9	43.8	2,711,113	17.3	48.9	2,446,739	15.5	46.9	2,425,501	13.2	45.2
9	5,531,841	36.2	100.0	5,544,072	35.4	100.0	5,213,669	33.0	100.0	5,368,843	29.1	100.0
10	109,525	0.7	1.6	103,303	0.7	1.4	134,469	0.8	1.7	151,145	0.8	1.5
11	360,320	2.4	5.2	348,227	2.2	4.7	358,263	2.3	4.6	537,200	2.9	5.5
12	197,838	1.3	2.8	186,344	1.2	2.5	211,716	1.3	2.7	278,312	1.5	2.8
13	2,167,876	14.2	31.2	2,838,872	18.1	38.1	2,351,390	14.9	30.2	3,092,708	16.8	31.4
14	1,365,848	9.0	19.7	1,166,971	7.5	15.7	1,512,908	9.6	19.4	2,036,996	11.0	20.7
15	4,201,407	27.5	60.5	4,643,717	29.7	62.3	4,568,476	28.9	58.7	6,096,361	33.0	61.9
16	492,067	3.2	7.1	535,299	3.4	7.2	540,828	3.4	7.0	575,029	3.1	5.8
17	47,660	0.3	0.7	46,109	0.3	0.6	55,169	0.3	0.7	72,219	0.4	0.7
18												
19	180,140	1.2	2.6	150,549	1.0	2.0	213,360	1.4	2.7	208,184	1.1	2.1
20	428,802	2.8	6.2	478,173	3.1	6.4	466,859	3.0	6.0	639,315	3.5	6.5
21	598,373	4.0	8.6	614,759	3.9	8.3	781,512	4.9	10.0	1,117,151	6.1	11.3
22	1,747,042	11.5	25.2	1,824,889	11.7	24.5	2,057,728	13.0	26.4	2,611,898	14.2	26.5
23	994,591	6.5	14.3	980,895	6.3	13.2	1,154,642	7.3	14.8	1,132,603	6.3	11.6
24	6,943,040	45.5	100.0	7,449,501	47.6	100.0	7,781,116	49.3	100.0	9,847,862	53.4	100.0
25	68,366	0.5	2.6	37,910	0.2	1.7	16,253	0.1	0.6	43,677	0.2	1.7
26	16,985	0.1	0.7	18,900	0.1	0.9	6,191	0.0	0.2	12,175	0.1	0.5
27	61,966	0.4	2.4	20,996	0.1	1.0	40,115	0.3	1.6	40,463	0.2	1.6
28	38,270	0.3	1.5	14,367	0.1	0.7	21,400	0.1	0.8	49,339	0.3	2.0
29	6,461	0.0	0.2				271	0.0	0.0	545	0.0	0.0
30	8,157	0.1	0.3	8,512	0.1	0.4	8,185	0.1	0.3	3,831	0.0	0.2
31	2,248	0.0	0.1	1,177	0.0	0.1	918	0.0	0.0	372	0.0	0.0
32	26,646	0.2	1.0	15,959	0.1	0.7	20,741	0.1	0.8	25,916	0.1	1.0
33	49,485	0.3	1.9	13,114	0.1	0.6	26,361	0.2	1.0	69,241	0.4	2.7
34	1,044	0.0	0.0	651	0.0	0.0	896	0.0	0.0	1,133	0.0	0.0
35	50,958	0.3	2.0	61,941	0.4	2.8	39,625	0.3	1.5	58,057	0.3	2.1

TABLE A-5 (continued)

	1966 Value	1966 % of Total	1966 % of Group	1967 Value	1967 % of Total	1967 % of Group	1968 Value	1968 % of Total	1968 % of Group	1969 Value	1969 % of Total	1969 % of Group
36	7,238	0.0	0.3	2,228	0.0	0.1	3,295	0.0	0.1	4,441	0.0	0.2
37	337,824	2.2	13.1	195,755	1.3	8.9	184,251	1.2	7.2	305,192	1.7	12.1
38	39,842	0.3	1.5	39,119	0.3	1.8	54,841	0.3	2.1	50,478	0.3	2.0
39	46,611	0.3	1.8	12,526	0.1	0.6	12,999	0.1	0.5	12,254	0.1	0.5
40	14,544	0.1	0.6	8,111	0.1	0.4	1,470	0.0	0.0	3,574	0.1	0.1
41	534,854	3.6	20.6	339,136	2.2	15.4	327,515	2.1	12.8	494,532	2.7	19.6
42	203,948	1.4	7.9	114,120	0.7	5.2	98,330	0.6	3.8	37,847	0.2	1.5
43	4,007	0.0	0.2	6,232	0.0	0.3	24,281	0.2	0.9	10,663	0.1	0.4
44	101,476	0.7	3.9	101,134	0.6	4.6	295,480	1.9	11.6	167,277	0.9	6.6
45	2,628	0.0	0.1	4,840	0.0	0.2	3,432	0.0	0.1	1,903	0.0	0.1
46	947,910	6.2	36.7	625,218	4.0	28.5	818,348	5.2	32.0	778,528	4.2	30.8
47	28,052	0.2	1.1	33,643	0.2	1.5	105,252	0.7	4.1	74,745	0.4	3.0
48	28,052	0.2	1.1	33,643	0.2	1.5	105,252	0.7	4.1	74,745	0.4	3.0
49	1,329	0.0	0.1	2,254	0.0	0.1	2,642	0.0	0.1	3,368	0.0	0.1
50	85,007	0.6	3.2	85,557	0.6	3.9	50,381	0.3	2.0	56,925	0.3	2.3
51	84,982	0.6	3.3	67,970	0.4	3.1	77,067	0.5	3.0	28,693	0.1	1.1
52	8	0.0	0.0	117	0.0	0.0	246	0.0	0.0	1,324	0.0	0.1
53	14,531	0.1	0.6	64,844	0.4	2.9	68,548	0.5	2.7	76,386	0.5	3.0
54	908	0.0	0.0	2,791	0.0	0.1	1,491	0.0	0.0	1,015	0.0	0.0
55	1,137	0.0	0.0	169	0.0	0.0	283	0.0	0.0	416	0.0	0.0
56	1,126	0.0	0.0	1,284	0.0	0.1	933	0.0	0.0	1,139	0.0	0.0
57	1,208	0.0	0.0	8,185	0.1	0.4	4,781	0.0	0.2	4,251	0.0	0.2
58	189,110	1.2	7.3	233,002	1.5	10.6	206,372	1.3	8.1	173,517	0.9	6.9
59	21,614	0.1	0.8	17,047	0.1	0.8	15,119	0.1	0.6	25,463	0.1	1.0
60	376,265	2.5	14.5	370,869	2.4	16.9	433,605	2.7	17.0	397,214	2.2	15.7
61	107,144	0.7	4.1	107,782	0.7	4.9	98,392	0.6	3.8	132,810	0.7	5.3
62	30,778	0.2	1.2	24,873	0.2	1.1	39,519	0.3	1.5	53,166	0.3	2.1
63	95,135	0.6	3.7	142,872	0.9	6.5	129,184	0.8	5.0	122,717	0.7	4.9
64	11,746	0.1	0.5	41,891	0.3	1.9	13,349	0.1	0.5	8,813	0.0	0.3
65	44,669	0.3	1.7	35,905	0.2	1.6	38,076	0.3	1.5	51,319	0.3	2.0
66	43,907	0.3	1.7	54,933	0.4	2.5	83,048	0.5	3.2	83,453	0.5	3.3
67	51,742	0.3	2.0	60,612	0.4	2.8	44,616	0.3	1.7	48,258	0.3	1.9
68	300,840	2.0	11.6	252,951	1.7	11.5	347,949	2.2	13.6	269,921	1.5	10.7
69	1,083,840	7.1	41.9	1,109,735	7.1	50.5	1,242,857	7.9	48.6	1,193,134	6.5	47.2
70	2,586,736	16.9	100.0	2,197,353	14.0	100.0	2,557,080	16.2	100.0	2,525,116	13.7	100.0

*1950, 1955, 1960-62 value in thousands of dinars (300 dinars = $1); 1964-69 value in thousands of new dinars (12.5 new dinars = $1).

Source: Statistika Spoljne Trgovine SFR Jugoslavije (Belgrade: Federal Institute for Statistics), 1961, pp. 21-23; 1963, pp. 23-24; 1966, pp. 24-25; 1969, pp. 26-27. Statistika Spoljne Trgovine FNR Jugoslavije (Belgrade: Federal Institute for Statistics), 1951, pp. xxii-xxiii; 1956, p. 20.

TABLE A-6

Imports by Country, 1950, 1955, 1960-69*
(country of payment)

Country	1950 Value	1950 % of Total	1950 % of Group	1955 Value	1955 % of Total	1955 % of Group	1960 Value	1960 % of Total	1960 % of Group	1961 Value	1961 % of Total	1961 % of Group	1962 Value	1962 % of Total	1962 % of Group
1 Albania							179	0.1	0.3	74	0.0	0.1	181	0.1	0.3
2 Bulgaria				396	0.3	4.1	3,123	1.2	4.8	3,568	1.3	6.9	3,471	1.3	6.1
3 Czechoslovakia				1,864	1.4	19.6	7,809	3.1	12.1	5,882	2.2	11.4	7,679	2.9	13.5
4 East Germany				630	0.5	6.6	11,197	4.5	17.4	11,279	4.1	21.9	10,907	4.1	19.1
5 Hungary				827	0.6	8.7	11,091	4.5	17.2	9,875	3.6	19.1	6,279	2.3	11.0
6 Poland				1,257	1.0	13.2	11,416	4.6	17.7	8,592	3.1	16.7	9,628	3.6	16.9
7 Rumania				175	0.1	1.8	2,490	1.0	3.9	2,285	0.8	4.4	1,055	0.4	1.9
8 USSR				4,373	3.3	45.9	17,098	6.9	26.5	10,032	3.7	19.4	17,806	6.7	31.2
9 Total Comecon				9,523	7.2	100.0	64,403	25.9	100.0	51,587	18.9	100.0	57,006	21.4	100.0
10 Belgium-Luxembourg	2,028	1.7	2.0	1,835	1.4	1.7	2,952	1.2	1.8	4,319	1.6	2.2	2,453	0.9	1.5
11 France	3,471	2.9	3.4	3,565	2.7	3.4	8,927	3.6	5.4	7,227	2.6	3.7	8,334	3.1	4.9
12 Netherlands	4,761	4.0	4.7	3,793	2.9	3.6	5,652	2.3	3.4	5,955	2.2	3.1	4,554	1.7	2.7
13 Italy	12,243	10.4	12.0	13,105	9.9	12.4	28,201	11.4	17.0	39,844	14.6	20.5	31,050	11.7	18.4
14 West Germany	19,455	16.5	19.0	16,810	12.7	15.9	36,056	14.5	21.8	42,843	15.7	22.0	30,200	11.4	18.0
15 Total EEC	41,958	35.6	41.0	39,108	29.6	37.0	81,788	33.0	49.4	100,178	36.7	51.4	76,591	28.8	45.7
16 Austria	9,028	7.6	8.8	5,663	4.3	5.4	11,106	4.5	6.7	9,624	3.5	4.9	9,677	3.6	5.7
17 Denmark	416	0.4	0.4	389	0.3	0.4	1,454	0.6	0.9	1,657	0.6	0.9	743	0.3	0.4
18 Portugal															
19 Sweden	1,590	1.4	1.6	1,156	0.9	1.1	2,592	1.1	1.6	2,860	1.1	1.5	2,999	1.1	1.8
20 Switzerland	4,043	3.4	4.0	4,075	3.1	3.9	5,786	2.3	3.5	7,215	2.6	3.7	5,015	1.9	3.0
21 UK	19,874	16.9	19.4	11,650	8.8	11.0	19,594	7.9	11.9	19,674	7.2	10.1	18,875	7.1	11.2
22 Total EFTA	34,951	29.6	34.2	22,933	17.3	21.7	40,532	16.3	24.5	41,030	15.0	21.1	37,309	14.0	22.1
23 United States	25,305	21.5	24.8	43,666	33.0	41.3	43,002	17.3	26.0	53,614	19.7	27.5	54,791	20.6	32.5
24 Total EEC, EFTA, and U.S.	102,214	86.7	100.0	105,707	79.9	100.0	165,322	66.7	100.0	194,822	71.3	100.0	168,691	63.3	100.0
25 Algeria				1	0.0	0.0	676	0.3	2.4	377	0.1	1.6	716	0.3	2.1
26 Ethiopia															
27 Ghana										61	0.0	0.3	473	0.2	1.4
28 Guinea										12	0.0	0.1	422	0.1	1.2
29 Ivory Coast															
30 Kenya															
31 Mali															
32 Morocco	40	0.0	0.3				318	0.1	1.1	548	0.2	2.3	460	0.1	1.4
33 Sudan							68	0.0	0.2	38	0.0	0.2	72	0.0	0.0
34 Liberia															
35 Tunisia				16	0.0	0.1	645	0.2	2.5	994	0.4	4.1	767	0.3	2.3

TABLE A-6 (Continued)

Country	1950 Value	1950 % of Total	1950 % of Group	1955 Value	1955 % of Total	1955 % of Group	1960 Value	1960 % of Total	1960 % of Group	1961 Value	1961 % of Total	1961 % of Group	1962 Value	1962 % of Total	1962 % of Group
36 Uganda															
37 Total Africa	40	0.0	0.3	17	0.0	0.1	1,707	0.7	6.2	2,030	0.7	8.4	2,910	1.1	8.6
38 Burma				82	0.1	0.6	929	0.4	3.3	350	0.1	1.5	498	0.2	1.5
39 Cambodia													99	0.0	0.3
40 Ceylon							92	0.0	0.3	330	0.1	1.4	38	0.0	0.1
41 India	57	0.1	0.4	5	0.0	0.0	2,540	1.0	9.2	2,375	0.9	9.9	6,767	2.5	19.9
42 Indonesia				241	0.2	1.9	159	0.1	0.6	358	0.1	1.5	1,440	0.6	4.2
43 Malaysia										74	0.0	0.3	312	0.1	0.9
44 Pakistan	343	0.3	2.4	419	0.3	3.3	1,519	0.6	5.5	1,423	0.5	5.9	486	0.2	1.4
45 Thailand							226	0.1	0.8	81	0.0	0.3	257	0.1	0.8
46 Total Asia	400	0.3	2.8	747	0.6	5.8	5,465	2.2	19.7	4,991	1.8	20.7	9,897	3.7	29.1
47 Spain							638	0.3	2.3	986	0.4	4.1	836	0.3	2.5
48 Total Europe	6,902	5.9	48.2				638	0.3	2.3	986	0.4	4.1	836	0.3	2.5
49 Argentina	678	0.6	4.7	486	0.4	3.8	610	0.2	2.2	1,810	0.6	7.5	1,937	0.7	5.7
50 Brazil				3,898	3.0	30.3	1,996	0.8	7.2	2,124	0.8	8.8	988	0.4	2.9
51 Cuba										591	0.2	2.4	1,498	0.6	4.4
52 Chile															
53 Colombia							211	0.1	0.8	887	0.1	3.7	603	0.2	1.8
54 Mexico	347	0.3	2.4	817	0.6	6.4				13	0.0	0.1			
55 Peru	26	0.0	0.2				368	0.2	1.3				4	0.0	0.0
56 Uruguay							412	0.2	1.5	261	0.1	1.1	170	0.1	0.5
57 Venezuela															
58 Total Latin and S. America	7,953	6.7	55.5	5,201	3.9	40.5	3,597	1.5	13.0	5,686	2.1	23.6	5,200	2.0	15.3
59 Cyprus				4	0.0	0.0	48	0.0	0.2	59	0.0	0.2	17	0.0	0.1
60 Greece				1,518	1.1	11.8	2,625	1.1	9.5	4,537	1.7	18.8	5,221	2.0	15.4
61 Iran	160	0.1	1.1							7	0.0	0.0	18	0.0	0.1
62 Iraq							51	0.0	0.2	306	0.1	1.3	1,680	0.6	4.9
63 Israel	86	0.1	0.6	1,122	0.8	8.7	1,363	0.6	4.9	1,715	0.7	7.1	2,914	1.1	8.6
64 Jordan							661	0.3	2.4	683	0.3	2.8	518	0.2	1.5
65 Lebanon				26	0.0	0.2	150	0.1	0.5	128	0.0	0.5	67	0.0	0.2
66 Libya															
67 Syria				58	0.0	0.5	16	0.0	0.1	82	0.0	0.3	133	0.1	0.4
68 Turkey	478	0.4	3.3	2,736	2.1	21.3	622	0.2	2.2	587	0.2	2.4	910	0.4	2.7
69 UAR	5,215	4.4	36.4	1,417	1.0	11.0	10,812	4.4	39.0	2,406	0.9	10.0	3,632	1.4	10.7
70 Total Middle East	5,939	5.0	41.4	6,881	5.2	53.6	16,348	6.6	58.9	10,410	3.8	43.2	15,110	5.7	44.5
71 Total Underdeveloped	14,332	12.2	100.0	12,846	9.7	100.0	27,755	11.2	100.0	24,103	8.8	100.0	33,953	12.7	100.0

Country	1963 Value	1963 % of Total	1963 % of Group	1964 Value	1964 % of Total	1964 % of Group	1965 Value	1965 % of Total	1965 % of Group
1	248	0.1	0.3	20,386	0.1	0.4	21,713	0.1	0.5
2	3,132	1.0	4.4	228,454	1.4	4.8	306,983	1.9	6.6
3	12,956	4.1	18.1	1,016,660	6.1	21.4	889,931	5.5	19.2
4	14,613	4.6	20.4	908,372	5.5	19.2	793,696	4.9	17.1
5	7,717	2.4	10.8	446,101	2.7	9.4	372,870	2.3	8.0
6	9,963	3.2	13.9	744,345	4.5	15.7	713,900	4.4	15.4
7	1,942	0.6	2.7	126,405	0.8	2.7	200,015	1.2	4.3
8	21,196	6.7	29.5	1,249,798	7.6	26.4	1,343,379	8.4	28.9
9	71,767	22.6	100.0	4,740,521	28.7	100.0	4,642,487	28.8	100.0
10	2,930	0.9	1.6	159,672	1.0	1.8	146,837	0.9	1.7
11	14,601	4.6	7.8	644,028	3.9	7.2	612,493	3.8	7.0
12	6,216	2.0	3.3	336,792	2.0	3.8	283,598	1.8	3.2
13	34,026	10.7	18.2	2,178,471	13.2	24.4	1,726,735	10.7	19.7
14	29,448	9.3	15.7	1,392,612	8.4	15.6	1,432,063	8.9	16.4
15	87,221	27.5	46.6	4,711,565	28.5	52.8	4,201,726	26.1	48.0
16	10,189	3.2	5.4	438,102	2.6	4.9	428,781	2.7	4.9
17	1,544	0.5	0.8	52,925	0.3	0.6	76,844	0.5	0.9
18									
19	3,925	1.2	2.1	200,829	1.2	2.3	181,616	1.1	2.1
20	7,074	2.2	3.8	317,683	1.9	3.6	301,706	1.9	3.5
21	21,234	6.7	11.3	1,041,428	6.3	11.7	1,106,702	6.9	12.7
22	43,966	13.9	23.5	2,050,967	12.4	23.0	2,095,649	13.1	24.0
23	56,032	17.7	29.9	2,160,230	13.0	24.2	2,447,517	15.2	28.0
24	187,219	59.1	100.0	8,922,762	53.9	100.0	8,744,892	54.3	100.0
25	1,210	0.4	2.8	75,315	0.5	3.2	34,794	0.2	1.7
26	1,064	0.3	2.5	48,623	0.3	2.1	30,712	0.2	1.5
27	1,538	0.5	3.6	48,501	0.3	2.1	62,625	0.4	3.0
28	402	0.1	0.9	11,805	0.1	0.5	29,914	0.2	1.4
29									
30				17,195	0.1	0.7	216	0.0	0.0
31				13,818	0.1	0.6	4,902	0.0	0.0
32	393	0.1	0.9	56,054	0.3	2.4	8,930	0.1	1.4
33	1,068	0.3	2.5	46,386	0.3	2.0	50,597	0.3	2.4
34									
35	674	0.2	1.6	49,485	0.3	2.1	78,313	0.5	3.8

146

TABLE A-6 (Continued)

Country	1963 Value	1963 % of Total	1963 % of Group	1964 Value	1964 % of Total	1964 % of Group	1965 Value	1965 % of Total	1965 % of Group
36				22,222	0.1	1.0	11,133	0.1	0.5
37	6,349	2.0	14.9	389,407	2.4	16.8	312,136	1.9	15.0
38	506	0.2	1.2	42,469	0.3	1.8	19,992	0.1	1.0
39	903	0.3	2.1	24,496	0.1	1.1	19,730	0.1	0.9
40	97	0.0	0.2	15,786	0.1	0.7	13,401	0.1	0.6
41	7,734	2.5	18.1	267,933	1.6	11.5	326,993	2.0	15.7
42	1,675	0.5	3.9	75,413	0.5	3.3	41,259	0.3	2.0
43	594	0.2	1.4	1,052	0.0	0.0	116	0.0	0.0
44	1,198	0.4	2.8	94,478	0.6	4.1	31,990	0.2	1.5
45	173	0.1	0.4	974	0.0	0.0	14,276	0.1	0.7
46	12,880	4.1	30.2	522,601	3.2	22.5	467,757	2.9	22.4
47	245	0.1	0.6	28,819	0.2	1.2	50,218	0.3	2.4
48	245	0.1	0.6	28,819	0.2	1.2	50,218	0.3	2.4
49	3,944	1.2	9.3	220,305	1.3	9.5	92,776	0.5	4.4
50	2,486	0.8	5.8	139,645	0.9	6.0	190,862	1.2	9.1
51	120	0.0	0.3	90,404	0.5	3.9	64,559	0.4	3.1
52	825	0.3	1.9	21,411	0.1	0.9	19,208	0.1	0.9
53				25,640	0.2	1.1	13,661	0.1	0.7
54	100	0.0	0.2	42,710	0.3	1.8	7,818	0.1	0.4
55	404	0.1	0.9	37,218	0.2	1.6	46,764	0.3	2.2
56	340	0.1	0.8	41,439	0.3	1.8	45,561	0.3	2.2
57									
58	8,219	2.6	19.2	618,772	3.7	26.1	481,219	3.0	23.1
59	90	0.0	0.2	8,870	0.0	0.4	2,094	0.0	0.1
60	3,689	1.2	8.7	130,164	0.8	5.6	210,438	1.3	10.1
61	291	0.1	0.6	40,069	0.2	1.7	6,943	0.1	0.3
62	1,934	0.6	4.5	43,837	0.3	1.9	9,789	0.1	0.5
63	2,000	0.6	4.7	119,937	0.7	5.2	119,645	0.7	5.7
64	687	0.2	1.6	36,414	0.2	1.6	35,328	0.2	1.7
65	117	0.0	0.3	4,206	0.0	0.2	3,534	0.0	0.2
66				3,346	0.0	0.1	8,603	0.1	0.4
67	173	0.1	0.4	27,577	0.2	1.2	6,902	0.1	0.3
68	705	0.2	1.7	56,313	0.3	2.4	70,000	0.4	3.4
69	5,230	1.7	12.3	289,167	1.8	12.5	301,727	1.9	14.5
70	14,916	4.7	35.0	760,400	4.6	32.7	775,003	4.8	37.7
71	42,609	13.4	100.0	2,319,999	14.0	100.0	2,086,333	13.0	100.0

147

TABLE A-6 (Continued)

Country	1966 Value	1966 % of Total	1966 % of Group	1967 Value	1967 % of Total	1967 % of Group	1968 Value	1968 % of Total	1968 % of Group	1969 Value	1969 % of Total	1969 % of Group
1	26,312	0.1	0.4	24,388	0.1	0.4	37,017	0.2	0.6	34,943	0.1	0.5
2	422,289	2.2	7.2	204,888	1.0	3.8	324,732	1.4	5.3	315,521	1.2	4.9
3	1,185,385	6.0	19.3	1,182,857	5.5	21.7	1,282,625	5.7	21.0	1,513,807	5.7	23.7
4	1,106,299	5.6	18.0	855,767	4.0	15.7	898,701	4.0	14.7	976,093	3.7	15.3
5	413,969	2.1	6.7	377,922	1.8	6.9	431,305	1.9	7.0	541,829	2.0	8.5
6	900,585	4.6	14.7	517,941	2.4	9.5	557,745	2.4	9.1	592,840	2.2	9.3
7	260,371	1.3	4.2	255,525	1.2	4.7	253,539	1.1	4.1	300,106	1.1	4.7
8	1,804,402	9.2	29.3	2,028,394	9.5	37.2	2,332,301	10.4	38.1	2,109,760	7.9	33.0
9	6,139,612	31.2	100.0	5,447,682	25.5	100.0	6,117,965	27.2	100.0	6,384,899	23.9	100.0
10	216,488	1.1	2.1	399,066	1.9	3.0	245,151	1.1	1.8	264,206	1.0	1.6
11	587,506	3.0	5.7	1,066,063	5.0	8.0	835,325	3.7	6.1	914,905	3.4	5.5
12	302,280	1.5	2.9	429,447	2.0	3.2	385,280	1.7	2.8	479,263	1.8	2.9
13	2,116,876	10.8	20.5	2,913,418	13.6	21.8	3,356,532	14.9	24.6	4,000,149	15.0	24.0
14	1,961,504	10.0	19.0	3,727,841	17.5	27.9	4,022,791	17.9	29.5	4,863,557	18.1	29.3
15	5,184,654	26.3	50.1	8,535,835	40.0	63.8	8,835,079	39.3	64.7	10,522,080	39.4	63.3
16	513,831	2.6	5.0	798,273	3.7	6.0	1,050,281	4.7	7.7	1,336,948	5.0	8.0
17	45,297	0.2	0.4	68,161	0.3	0.5	88,602	0.4	0.6	104,556	0.4	0.6
18												
19	159,454	0.8	1.5	230,878	1.1	1.7	253,979	1.1	1.9	382,158	1.4	2.3
20	446,387	2.3	4.3	633,816	3.0	4.7	813,496	3.6	6.0	1,245,341	4.7	7.5
21	1,490,848	7.7	14.4	1,531,512	7.2	11.4	1,455,307	6.5	10.7	1,939,497	7.3	11.7
22	2,655,817	13.5	25.7	3,262,640	15.3	24.4	3,661,665	16.3	26.8	5,008,500	18.8	30.0
23	2,501,633	12.7	24.2	1,586,039	7.4	11.8	1,144,003	5.1	8.4	1,096,262	4.2	6.6
24	10,343,104	52.5	100.0	13,384,514	62.7	100.0	13,640,747	60.7	100.0	16,626,842	62.3	100.0
25	18,514	0.1	0.8	40,027	0.2	1.6	50,565	0.2	2.2	49,121	0.2	1.4
26	12,392	0.1	0.5	13,357	0.1	0.5	7,096	0.0	0.3	21,017	0.1	0.6
27	66,491	0.3	2.8	60,510	0.3	2.4	48,745	0.2	2.1	57,091	0.2	1.6
28	48,987	0.3	2.1	34,749	0.2	1.4	32,872	0.2	1.4	24,016	0.1	0.7
29												
30	182	0.0	0.6	303	0.0	0.0	12,029	0.1	0.5	22,480	0.1	0.6
31	14,900	0.1	0.6	5,739	0.0	0.2	17,630	0.1	0.8	15,891	0.0	0.4
32	27,602	0.1	1.2	17,279	0.1	0.7	17,360	0.1	0.7	44,306	0.2	1.2
33	8,799	0.1	0.4	3,712	0.0	0.1	26,852	0.1	1.2	51,085	0.2	1.4
34												
35	75,769	0.4	3.2	75,273	0.4	3.0	66,849	0.3	2.9	77,341	0.3	2.2

TABLE A-6 (Continued)

Country	1966 Value	1966 % of Total	1966 % of Group	1967 Value	1967 % of Total	1967 % of Group	1968 Value	1968 % of Total	1968 % of Group	1969 Value	1969 % of Total	1969 % of Group
36	273,636	1.4	11.6	251,029	1.2	10.0	112	0.0	0.0	16,598	0.1	0.5
37	22,806	0.1	1.0	7,244	0.0	0.3	280,110	1.2	12.1	378,946	1.4	10.6
38	4,815	0.0	0.2	389	0.0	0.0	230	0.0	0.0	32,506	0.1	0.9
39	4,574	0.0	0.2	7,382	0.0	0.3	25,577	0.1	1.1	4,149	0.0	0.1
40	318,246	1.6	13.4	278,541	1.3	11.1	9,420	0.0	0.4	12,547	0.0	0.4
41	69,105	0.4	2.9	2,428	0.0	0.1	252,207	1.1	10.9	434,810	1.6	12.2
42	3,908	0.0	0.2	88,951	0.4	3.5	11,445	0.1	0.5	9,108	0.0	0.3
43	25,235	0.1	1.1	82,389	0.4	3.3	84,717	0.4	3.7	158,819	0.6	4.4
44	11,643	0.1	0.5	24,601	0.1	1.0	73,096	0.3	3.2	141,105	0.5	4.0
45	460,332	2.3	19.4	491,925	2.3	19.6	13,266	0.1	0.5	14,153	0.1	0.4
46	45,317	0.2	3.3	44,692	0.2	1.8	469,958	2.1	20.3	807,197	3.0	22.6
47	45,317	0.2	3.3	44,692	0.2	1.8	88,729	0.4	3.8	224,448	0.8	6.3
48	127,180	0.6	5.4	144,386	0.7	5.8	88,729	0.4	3.8	224,448	0.8	6.3
49	216,794	1.1	9.2	257,063	1.2	10.3	57,760	0.3	2.5	79,917	0.3	2.2
50	114,548	0.6	4.8	51,105	0.2	2.0	182,068	0.8	7.9	255,648	1.0	7.2
51	91,148	0.5	3.9	54,102	0.2	2.2	64,715	0.3	2.8	37,905	0.1	1.1
52	20,124	0.1	0.8	23,306	0.1	0.9	21,685	0.1	0.9	17,461	0.1	0.5
53	1,229	0.0	0.1	2,633	0.0	0.1	62,219	0.3	2.7	50,879	0.2	1.4
54	78,961	0.4	3.3	72,973	0.3	2.9	1,970	0.0	0.1	14,349	0.1	0.4
55	21,600	0.1	0.9	15,052	0.1	0.6	77,520	0.3	3.3	88,325	0.3	2.5
56				19,888	0.1	0.8	10,970	0.1	0.5	7,786	0.0	0.2
57							24,741	0.1	1.1	21,046	0.1	0.6
58	671,584	3.4	28.4	640,508	3.0	25.6	503,648	2.2	21.7	573,326	2.1	16.0
59	1,908	0.0	0.1	3,254	0.0	0.1	7,809	0.0	0.3	2,225	0.0	0.1
60	341,230	1.7	14.4	382,226	1.8	15.3	311,114	1.4	13.4	417,109	1.6	11.7
61	2,032	0.0	0.1	85,659	0.4	3.4	35,091	0.2	1.5	223,826	0.8	6.3
62	152,272	0.8	6.4	91,101	0.4	3.6	150,017	0.7	6.5	234,016	0.9	6.6
63	49,597	0.3	2.0	128,507	0.6	5.1	116,522	0.5	5.0	109,571	0.4	3.1
64	8,416	0.0	0.4	28,977	0.2	1.2	41,561	0.2	1.8	55,960	0.2	1.6
65	7,506	0.0	0.3	15,180	0.1	0.6	23,201	0.1	1.0	35,420	0.2	1.0
66	2,860	0.0	0.1	88,327	0.4	3.5	64,120	0.3	2.8	21,833	0.1	0.6
67				1,635	0.0	0.1				48,971	0.2	1.4
68	43,897	0.2	1.9	26,204	0.1	1.0	27,428	0.1	1.2	67,988	0.3	1.9
69	305,561	1.6	12.9	223,272	1.0	8.9	196,560	0.9	8.5	371,383	1.4	10.4
70	915,279	4.6	38.7	1,074,342	5.0	42.9	973,423	4.3	42.0	1,587,301	6.0	44.4
71	2,366,148	12.0	100.0	2,502,496	11.7	100.0	2,315,868	10.3	100.0	3,571,208	13.4	100.0

*1950, 1955, 1960-63 value in thousands of dinars (300 dinars = $1); 1964-69 value in thousands of new dinars (12.5 new dinars = $1).

Source: Statistika Spoljne Trgovine SFR Jugoslavije, (Belgrade: Federal Institute for Statistics), 1964, pp. 24-25; 1965, pp. 26-27; 1969, pp. 24-25. Statistika Spoljne Trgovine FNR Jugoslavije, (Belgrade: Federal Institute for Statistics), 1951, pp. xx-xxi; 1957, p. 21.

TABLE A-7

Bloc Participation in World Trade by Countries
(Value in Million $ U.S.)

Country	1948	1953	1959	1960	1961	1962	1963	1964	1965	1966	1967
Exports (f.o.b.)[g]											
Albania[b]			85	81	72	65	71	98			
Bulgaria[e]		200	580	633	666	785	933	1,062	1,178	1,478	1,572
Czechoslovakia[b]	681	879	1,602	1,816	2,024	2,070	2,160	2,429	2,673	2,736	2,680
E. Germany[b,c,d]		920	1,783	1,918	2,047	2,212	2,133	2,377	2,546	2,865	2,972
Hungary	167	488	793	976	1,026	1,149	1,306	1,495	1,521	1,566	1,776
Poland[b]	516	774	1,420	1,495	1,687	1,885	1,979	2,072	2,340	2,494	2,645
Rumania[d,e]		395	502	648	815	942	1,022	1,168	1,077	1,213	1,546
USSR	368		5,073	5,630	5,828	6,455	7,055	7,736	8,058	7,913	8,536
Yugoslavia[a]		186	687	826	910	888	1,057	1,323	1,288	1,575	1,707
Eastern Europe and USSR	1,732	3,656	12,525	14,023	15,075	16,451	17,720	19,760	20,681	21,840	23,444
Imports (c.i.f.)[g]											
Albania[b]			34	49	49	41	48	60			
Bulgaria[e]		206	467	572	663	778	834	980	1,176	1,305	1,458
Czechoslovakia[b]	753	994	1,727	1,930	2,046	2,194	2,462	2,576	2,689	2,745	2,864
E. Germany[b]		706	1,913	1,966	2,062	2,167	2,470	2,667	2,776	2,898	3,159
Hungary	166	498	770	874	1,029	1,100	1,206	1,352	1,510	1,594	1,720
Poland[b,c,d]	533	831	1,145	1,326	1,504	1,646	1,770	2,096	2,228	2,272	2,527
Rumania[d,e]			523	717	793	818	915	1,000	1,102	1,186	1,395
USSR			5,450	5,564	5,998	7,031	7,272	7,683	8,175	8,841	9,649
Yugoslavia[a]	304	186	477	566	569	691	790	893	1,092	1,220	1,252
Eastern Europe and USSR	1,076	3,421	12,506	13,564	14,713	16,461	17,767	19,307	20,748	22,061	24,006

[a] The figures for Yugoslavia exclude goods imported into customs bond and re-exported without being cleared for domestic production, whereas all the others include such goods.

[b] Imports—f.o.b.

[c] Excludes trade with West Germany.

[d] Prior to 1959, special trade.

[e] Beginning 1959, imports f.o.b.

[f] Imports—f.o.b.

[g] Beginning 1953, data have been converted from national currencies, which have official parities with the USSR ruble, into U.S. dollar at .90 USSR new ruble to a U.S. dollar.

Source: United Nations Statistical Yearbook (New York: United Nations, 1969), p. 392, 393.

TABLE A-8

Yugoslavia's Bloc Balance of Trade, 1960-69

Year	Balance of Trade*								
	Albania	Bulgaria	Czech.	E. Germany	Hungary	Poland	Rumania	USSR	Total Bloc
1960	-3,465	-15,427	-6,971	93,513	-207,900	-198,948	-48,840	-26,647	-414,662
1961	-948	-48,922	-33,578	-131,959	-187,110	146,437	34,732	252,243	30,896
1962	-990	-72,353	-55,440	-28,586	-123,503	126,266	44,220	-186,656	297,041
1963	-6,476	-19,181	-247,417	-137,197	-167,887	61,999	-19,181	185,666	-349,717
1964	-9,729	-104,981	-456,451	-117,763	-147,588	-248,953	-3,887	205,779	-883,573
1965	989	-89,965	-2,135	156,033	-49,543	89,445	-39,584	1,000,383	1,065,623
1966	-1,746	-282,560	-340,715	-303,628	-48,166	-196,734	-51,668	617,446	-607,771
1967	9,990	120	-558,645	-74,264	-41,896	54,422	23,949	682,719	96,389
1968	-19,061	258	-604,422	-233,068	-75,405	-95,781	8,745	114,438	-904,296
1969	2,793	-90,472	-736,580	-466,209	793	-7,055	-35,067	315,741	-1,016,056
1960-69	-28,643	-723,483	-3,042,354	-1,243,128	-1,048,205	-268,902	-86,581	3,161,112	-3,280,208

EXPORTS/IMPORTS

Year	Albania	Bulgaria	Czech.	E. Germany	Hungary	Poland	Rumania	USSR	Total Bloc
1960	53.1	88.0	97.8	120.2	54.6	57.8	52.4	96.2	84.5
1961	68.9	66.8	86.2	71.6	54.1	141.3	136.8	161.0	101.5
1962	86.7	49.5	82.5	93.7	45.2	131.8	201.6	74.6	87.4
1963	36.7	85.2	53.7	77.2	47.3	115.1	76.1	121.2	88.2
1964	52.3	54.0	55.1	87.0	66.9	66.6	96.9	116.5	81.4
1965	104.6	70.7	99.8	119.7	86.7	112.5	80.2	174.5	123.2
1966	93.4	36.1	71.3	72.6	88.4	78.2	80.2	134.2	90.1
1967	141.0	100.1	52.8	91.3	88.9	110.5	109.4	133.7	101.8
1968	48.5	100.1	52.9	74.1	82.5	82.8	103.4	104.9	85.2
1969	108.0	71.3	51.3	52.2	100.1	98.8	88.3	115.0	84.1

*Value in thousands of new dinars (12.5 n.d.=$1).

Source: Appendix A, Table, A-5 and A-6.

151

INSTRUMENTS REGULATING COMMODITY
EXCHANGE BETWEEN YUGOSLAVIA AND
THE MEMBERS OF COMECON*

U.S.S.R.

The Trade and Payments Agreements of January 5, 1955 (with changes and supplements to be agreed upon by both parties during the validity of the Trade Agreement).

Both agreements are valid for one year, and are tacitly extended from year to year unless cancelled by one of the parties three months before expiration.

The Agreement on long-term commodity exchange of May 19, 1966. This agreement stipulates basic products to be exchanged during the 1966-1970 period.

The Protocol on Commodity Exchange for 1967 of October 29, 1966, stipulating the exchange for 1967.

The Protocol on Industrial Co-operation of March 1963.

The Agreement on Air Traffic on September 3, 1955.

The Agreement on the transportation of commodities between the USSR and Yugoslavia and on transit through Hungary by railways, of April 10, 1965.

The Agreement on the formation of the Inter-Governmental Yugoslav-Soviet Committee for Economic Co-operation of June 7, 1965.

---

*Yugoslav Foreign Trade Almanac (Belgrade: Yugoslaviapublic, 1968), pp. 107-9.

POLAND

The Trade and Payments Agreements of February 12, 1965 providing for basic instruments regulating commodity exchange and payments. The Payments Agreement foresees the clearing account and mutual revolving credit. Both agreements are valid for one year and are tacitly extended each year unless cancelled by one of the parties three months before expiration.

The Long-Term Agreement on Mutual Deliveries of Goods for the 1966-1970 period, signed on April 29, 1966. The Agreement foresees basic products to be exchanged during this period, determining the quantities and values of these goods, whereas each year detailed commodity lists will be stipulated. The Agreement also includes mutual deliveries of products on the basis of industrial co-operation.

The Proctocol on Commodity Exchange for 1967 signed on October 24, 1966 in Warsaw. The Protocol incorporates commodity lists with corresponding quotas for 1967.

The Agreement on Scientific and Technical Co-operation of November 14, 1955.

The Tourist Arrangement of February 18, 1959.

The Agreement on Industrial Co-operation of November 12, 1957.

The Agreement providing for the establishment of the Yugoslav-Polish Committee for Economic Co-operation, of February 20, 1958.

CZECHOSLOVAKIA

The Protocol on Commodity Exchange signed on October 9, 1966 for 1967.

The Protocol on Long-Term Commodity Exchange for the 1965-1970 period, signed in February 1965.

The Payments Agreement signed between the Governments of Yugoslavia and Czechlosovakia on May 9, 1964, automatically extended unless cancelled by one of the parties concerned within an agreed upon term.

The Agreement providing for co-operation in the field of nonferrous and iron and steel industry, signed between the Yugoslav
Investment Bank and the Ministry of Foreign Trade of Czechoslovakia on May 15, 1965.

The Protocol on Co-operation between Yugoslav and Czechoslovak
traders and producers on the third markets, of June 22, 1963.

The Tourist Agreement of March 4, 1964.

THE DEMOCRATIC REPUBLIC OF GERMANY

The Agreement on Trade and Services of December 22, 1958.

The Payments Agreement of October 19, 1957. Both agreements
are automatically extended each year unless cancelled at a three
months notice of termination.

The Payments Agreement foresees clearing payments in US
dollars and a mutual revolving credit.

The Protocol on Long-Term Commodity Exchange of February
28, 1966 for the 1966-1970 period. The Protocol serves as a
basis to establish annual exchange of goods.

HUNGARY

The Agreement on mutual deliveries of goods during the 1966-
1970 period.

The Payments Agreement of June 26, 1956.

The Protocol on Commodity Exchange for 1966 of November 21,
1965 with commodity lists for 1966 attached to it.

The Agreement on Long-Term Commodity Exchange of April 1,
1966 providing for basic articles to be exchanged during the
1966-1970 period.

The Agreement on the establishment of Yugoslav-Hungarian
Committee for Economic Co-operation of March 27, 1963.

RUMANIA

The Trade and Payments Agreements of October 27, 1956. The
Payments Agreement provides for clearing payments and mutual

revolving credit. The agreements are automatically extended
from year to year.

The Protocol on Long-Term Commodity Exchange for the 1966-
1970 period, signed on April 7, 1966, incorporating commodity
lists.

The Protocol on Commodity Exchange for 1967 of November 1,
1966.

BULGARIA

The Trade and Payments Agreement of March 16, 1955. The
Agreement provides for the establishment of commodity lists
for each year and for the possibility of contracting compensation
agreement irrespective of the quotas foreseen by the commodity
lists.

The Payments Agreement provides for a clearing account.

The Trade and Payments Agreement as well as the revolving
credit are tacitly extended each year unless cancelled at least
three months before expiration.

The Agreement on Long-Term Commodity Exchange for the
1966-1970 period. The Agreement includes prospective commodity lists.

ALBANIA

The Trade and Payments Agreement of May 17, 1955. The
Protocol on Commodity Exchange for 1966 extends the validity
of the Trade and Payments Agreement of May 17, 1955 and
complies with the provisions of this Agreement. The Payments
Agreement provides for a clearing account in US dollars and for
a revolving credit. Both Agreements are automatically extended
each year unless cancelled by one of the contracting party in the
stipulated term.

THE DATA

All calculations were made from official Yugoslav data reported in the Yugoslav trade yearbook (Statistika Spoljne Trgovine SFR Jugoslavije). Items that accounted for less than 300,000 dinars of trade were excluded from the calculations. This allowed the exclusion of up to 75 percent of the items with only a small loss in the dinar value. Table C-1 reports the percentage of the total value of trade that was included in these price calculations. The Western price standard was calculated as a mean of the average unit values in trade with the three most important Western sources (buyers) of that item. In all instances the first choice in the unit value comparisons were unit values calculated on the same item (the same seven-digit SITC number). In a few cases where Yugoslavia did not trade an item with both areas this was impossible. In these instances the first alternative was to use the import unit value from Western markets as a standard for the export unit value to the bloc. Conversely

TABLE C-1

Value of Selected Bundle as Percent of
Total Bundle, 1966-68

Country	1966	1967	1968
Albania	89.2	90.1	91.4
Bulgaria	92.1	91.8	93.5
Czechoslovakia	84.0	90.3	96.1
E. Germany	87.6	91.8	95.1
Hungary	91.4	88.2	92.9
Poland	94.8	94.1	93.2
Rumania	90.7	94.2	93.7
USSR	96.8	97.1	97.4

the Western export unit value was compared to the bloc import unit
value. The second alternative was to use a six-digit SITC number
item as the standard. In some cases where an "acceptable" comparison was impossible the item was excluded. The decision on
whether or not to exclude some of these items was by necessity arbi-
trary. Table C-1 arrays the size of the bundle subjected to the calculations as a percent of the total bundle and Table C-2 presents
the results of these calculations (see Chapter 6).

TABLE C-2

Measures of Discrimination[a]

Country	Year	Overcharge on Exports[b]	Underpayment on Imports[c]	Total Discrimination[d]	Total Value of Trade[e]	Monopoly Gain of State Trading[f]
Albania						
	1968	2,905	-123,267	126,172	1,339,249	29.0
	1967	1,415	-122,351	123,766	1,473,335	29.8
	1966	7,487	-93,517	101,004	2,506,702	36.0
	1966-68					32.5
Bulgaria						
	1968	6,294	-167,187	173,482	723,336	37.6
	1967	132	-99,822	99,954	731,489	31.1
	1966	-2,215	-191,337	189,122	890,698	52.2
	1966-68					41.1
Czechoslovakia						
	1968	82,404	-153,677	1,619,171	6,504,453	24.5
	1967	82,846	-782,538	865,383	5,471,369	14.5
	1966	-103,980	-834,922	730,942	5,185,761	20.2
	1966-68					20.0
E. Germany						
	1968	58,439	-540,235	598,674	16,099,763	33.3
	1967	61,230	-438,474	499,704	13,836,514	24.3
	1966	-49,611	-510,082	460,471	15,243,837	28.2
	1966-68					28.8
Hungary						
	1968	36,731	-561,193	597,925		
	1967	43,827	-264,859	308,686	9,595,311	39.4
	1966	-108,835	-514,217	405,382	8,365,146	30.6
	1966-68				10,058,076	32.3
						34.2
Poland						
	1968	106,286	-282,297	388,583	170,632	73.9
	1967	3,911	-435,182	439,093	177,482	69.7
	1966	60,178	-840,474	900,652	146,411	69.0
	1966-68					71.0
Rumania						
	1968	43,523	-228,492	272,016	768,078	22.6
	1967	17,856	-209,274	227,130	542,965	18.4
	1966	-67,406	-532,440	465,034	829,226	22.8
	1966-68					21.6
Soviet Union						
	1968	-3,915	-1,595,292	1,591,376	3,354,537	48.3
	1967	-20,321	-815,648	795,327	2,497,956	34.6
	1966	-459,135	-1,504,473	1,045,338	2,435,035	30.0
	1966-68					38.8
Total Comecon						
	1968			5,367,399	1,983,015	30.2
	1967			5,359,043	2,003,020	25.0
	1966			4,297,945	2,131,597	21.6
	1966-68					25.5
Total Comecon (Except USSR)						
	1968			5,776,023	1,256,463	47.6
	1967			2,563,716	938,899	32.9
	1966			5,252,607	1,118,407	36.2
	1966-68					39.6

[a] Values in thousands new dinars (12.5 new dinars = \$1).

[b] $\sum_{j=1}^{n} Q_j xr (P_j xr - P_j xw)$, see Chapter 5 for notation.

[c] $\sum_{k=1}^{m} Q_k mr (P_k mr - P_k mw)$

[d] $\pi = \sum_{j=1}^{m} Q_j xr (P_j xr - P_j xw) - \sum_{k=1}^{m} Q_k mr (P_k mr - P_k mw)$

[e] $\sum_{j=1}^{n} Q_j xr P_j xw + \sum_{k=1}^{m} Q_k mr P_k mw$

[f] Column 3/ column 4.

TABLE D-1

Percentage Share of SITC Sections 6-8 in the
Trade Bundle of Yugoslavia*

Country	Year	Exports	Imports
Albania			
	1968	85.7	17.6
	1967	73.5	1.7
	1966	63.3	12.3
Bulgaria			
	1968	46.8	33.3
	1967	44.1	29.8
	1966	39.8	36.9
Czechoslovakia			
	1968	69.0	84.4
	1967	67.3	83.0
	1966	71.6	82.9
E. Germany			
	1968	76.1	81.0
	1967	57.7	77.8
	1966	60.9	76.7
Hungary			
	1968	62.7	69.4
	1967	73.6	69.1
	1966	69.5	81.6
Poland			
	1968	76.6	80.3
	1967	84.7	80.2
	1966	71.8	82.2
Rumania			
	1968	82.2	55.3
	1967	70.8	50.8
	1966	78.3	48.6
USSR			
	1968	78.3	44.4
	1967	79.2	43.1
	1966	79.1	50.9

*Percentage share as measured from the bundle used to calculate the measure of discrimination. See Appendix C for a discussion of the selection of this bundle. SITC sections 6-8 are Manufactured Goods by Material, Machinery and Transport Equipment, and Miscellaneous Manufactured Goods, respectively.

SITC[a] Section Measures of Discrimination
(as a percent of hypothetical bundle) [b]

Exports		0	1	2	3	4	5	6	7	8
Albania	1968	-28.9		-60.2			13.2	-5.3	262.9	-51.2
	1967				44.1		3.5	4.9		2.1
	1966						34.6	74.1	76.6	
Bulgaria	1968	6.6	8.9	-25.4			-24.0	34.2	44.7	58.8
	1967	-11.5	-5.9	4.8			-15.3	42.0	-13.4	13.4
	1966	-17.4		13.3			10.1	27.8	-17.6	46.8
Czechoslovakia	1968	5.6	17.0	1.6	39.3	-6.6	-51.5	32.4	18.9	21.1
	1967	3.3	45.2	59.7	30.4	12.1	-0.9	20.5	3.2	55.3
	1966	-21.5	10.2	35.5	18.0		-36.7	3.0	-39.4	52.0
E. Germany	1968	12.9	17.2	53.0	43.2		35.6	9.2	-5.2	79.5
	1967	23.8	27.5	44.9		-83.3	5.1	-28.4	11.6	71.4
	1966	-1.5	5.8	28.9			-3.0	11.4	-40.1	87.6
Hungary	1968	39.8	46.9	18.7	33.8		-22.0	2.7	16.4	94.1
	1967	46.1	33.8	27.6	41.9		30.7	21.6	0.6	91.5
	1966	-38.3	2.3	-21.3	84.2		-52.2	43.6	-54.7	76.7
Poland	1968	9.0	32.3	15.8	39.0		43.4	63.0	1.6	59.4
	1967	36.9	53.5	19.9	35.7		35.9	34.1	-23.1	83.7
	1966	7.5	10.8	29.7	17.2		-39.1	95.7	-26.4	79.2
Rumania	1968	-10.5	26.7	73.1			64.5	23.0	-18.7	12.2
	1967	0.9	79.6	60.4			22.6	13.7	-29.1	78.9
	1966	0.7	4.5	16.8			-53.9	31.2	-59.0	129.0
Soviet Union	1968	-7.5	24.3	-10.3	31.8		-3.8	30.9	-12.6	0.3
	1967	51.8	-3.1	-38.1	27.0		-16.6	5.9	-26.5	66.2
	1966	-62.8	17.7	-37.1	16.4		-44.3	25.7	-27.6	88.2
Imports										
Albania	1968	18.6	205.9	-86.7	35.4		3.2	15.6	-13.3	
	1967		-83.3	-86.6	-3.4		-6.4	-8.4	-84.8	
	1966	-36.5	58.8	-85.6	-57.8		-62.2		-16.9	
Bulgaria	1968	-5.4		36.9	6.8	16.5	-72.6	-25.2	- 5.3	-21.4
	1967	-9.4	-41.1	-58.2	17.4		-51.9	-13.3	-58.0	36.2
	1966	-28.7	-67.8	-22.1	-62.8		-10.7	-25.7	12.2	15.7
Czechoslovakia	1968	8.5	-3.2	-50.1	-20.9	0.5	-69.0	-22.5	-67.4	-48.9
	1967	-14.1	-24.8	-47.0	-16.3	27.8	-49.7	-26.8	-39.5	-76.5
	1966	1.0		-80.1	-24.3	18.6	-42.0	-27.5	-46.2	-70.7
E. Germany	1968	5.8	0.5	-33.3	-52.5	-16.5	33.3	-27.6	-43.8	-47.0
	1967	-15.7	-53.8	-20.5	-3.2	193.9	-35.5	-18.0	-32.1	-64.3
	1966	6.2	-42.9	-28.5	-20.9	32.0	-40.4	-21.5	-35.1	-47.0
Hungary	1968	-62.7		-86.8	-39.6		-24.7	-46.5	-74.7	-47.8
	1967	-63.7		-19.0	-19.9		14.4	-43.4	-34.0	-64.8
	1966	-60.4		-2.7	-78.6		27.1	-61.4	-28.4	-72.6
Poland	1968	-1.3	23.9	-22.9	-1.6		-46.1	-32.7	-40.5	-42.2
	1967	-74.3	-56.6	-33.4	-56.0		-42.6	-40.3	-51.5	-20.1
	1966	-72.4		-79.9	-77.7		-67.1	-30.6	-37.2	-63.7
Rumania	1968	-0.1	68.6	-77.9	-19.7		-79.3	-44.5	-47.0	-51.7
	1967	-26.8		-87.6	-38.5		-36.7	-7.5	-65.6	-84.8
	1966	-47.5		-92.8	-68.9		-23.8	-65.4	-57.7	-46.8
Soviet Union	1968	-18.5	29.4	-26.0		20.9	-40.4	-59.2	-56.4	-43.8
	1967	-15.7	-42.0	-37.0	-34.2	31.5	-31.6	-3.5	-50.0	-51.9
	1966	10.0	-48.2	-78.9	-39.2	-34.5	-65.6	-15.7	-42.4	-50.9

[a] 0- Food and Live Animals; 1- Beverages and Tobacco; 2- Crude Materials, Inedible, except Fuels;
3- Mineral Fuels, Lubricants and Related Materials; 4- Animal and Vegetable Oils and Fats;
5- Chemicals; 6- Manufactured Goods by Material; 7- Machinery and Transport Equipment; 8- Miscellaneous Manufactured Goods

[b]

$$\sum_{j=1}^{n} Q_j^{xr} \left(P_j^{xr} - P_j^{xw} \right) \Bigg/ \sum_{j=1}^{n} Q_j^{xr} P_j^{xw} \text{ for exports, } \sum_{k=1}^{m} Q_k^{mr} \left(P_k^{mr} - P_k^{mw} \right) \Bigg/$$

$$\sum_{k=1}^{m} Q_k^{mr} P_k^{mw} \text{ for imports. See Chapter 5 for notation.}$$

BIBLIOGRAPHY

BOOKS AND PAMPHLETS

Adler-Karlsson, Gunnar. Western Economic Warfare 1947-1967. Stockholm: Almquist and Wicksell, 1968.

Allen, Robert Loring. Soviet Economic Warfare. Washington: Public Affairs Press, 1960.

Ames, Edward. Soviet Economic Processes. Homewood, Ill.: Richard D. Irwin, 1965.

Avakumovic, Ivan. History of the Communist Party of Yugoslavia. Aberdeen: The Aberdeen University Press, 1964.

Balassa, Bela A. The Hungarian Experience in Economic Planning. New Haven, Conn.: Yale University Press, 1959.

Baumol, William J. Economic Dynamics. New York: The Macmillan Company, 1951.

_____. Economic Theory and Operations Analysis. Englewood Cliffs, N.J.: Prentice-Hall, 1965.

Bilandzic, Dusan. Management of Yugoslav Economy, 1945-1966. Translated by Jelena Hercog. Belgrade: Yugoslav Trade Unions, 1967.

Bogosavljevic, Milutin. The Economy of Yugoslavia. Translated by Nina Arneri. Belgrade: International Labor Exchange, 1961.

Bombelles, Joseph T. Economic Development of Communist Yugoslavia, 1947-1964. Stanford, Calif.: Hoover Institution Publications, 1968.

Bornstein, Morris (ed.). Comparative Economic System. Homewood, Ill.: Richard D. Irwin, 1969.

Brown, Alan and E. Neuberger (eds.). International Trade and Central Planning. Los Angeles: University of California Press, 1968.

171

Brzezinski, Zbigniew. The Soviet Bloc. Cambridge, Mass.: Harvard
University Press, 1960.

Clabaugh, Samuel F. and Edwin J. Feulner. Trading with the Communists. Washington, D.C.: The Center for Strategic Studies,
1968.

Clissold, Stephen (ed.). A Short History of Yugoslavia. Cambridge:
At the University Press, 1966.

Colanovic, Branko. Development of the Underdeveloped Areas of
Yugoslavia. Belgrade: Medunarodna Politika, 1966.

Coppock, Joseph D. International Economic Instability. New York:
McGraw-Hill Book Company, 1962.

Crvenkovski, Krste. Jugoslavia: Along New Paths. Translated by
Bosko Milosavljevic. Belgrade: Nemanjina 34, 1967.

Cvorovic, Mirceta and Milan Ristic. Yugoslavia in the System of
Multilateral International Economic Cooperation. Belgrade:
Interpress, 1967.

Dell, Sidney. Trade Blocs and Common Markets. New York: Alfred
A. Knopf, 1963.

Dewar, Margaret. Soviet Trade with Eastern Europe, 1945-1949.
London: Royal Institute of International Affairs, 1951.

Dickinson, H. D. Economics of Socialism. London: Oxford University Press, 1939.

Eckstein, Alexander. Communist China's Economic Growth and
Foreign Trade. New York: McGraw-Hill Book Company, 1966.

Fellner, William. Competition Among the Few. New York: Alfred
A. Knopf, 1949.

Flek, Josef; Lubomir Kruzik, and Bedrich Levcik. Economic Competition Between Capitalism and Socialism. Translated by
Gene Nemcova. Prague: Publishing House for Political Literature, 1962.

Foreign Area Studies Division. Area Handbook for Yugoslavia. Washington, D.C.: Special Operations Research Office, American
University, 1959.

Garmarnikov, Michael. Economic Reforms in Eastern Europe.
    Detroit: Wayne State University Press, 1968.

Goldman, Marshall I. Comparative Economic Systems: A Reader.
    New York: Random House, 1964.

_____. Soviet Foriegn Aid. New York: Praeger, 1967.

Gruchy, Alan. Comparative Economic Systems. Boston: Houghton
    Mifflin Company, 1966.

Hamilton, F. E. Ian. Yugoslavia: Patterns of Economic Activity.
    London: G. Bell and Sons, 1968.

Harvey, Mose L. East West Trade and United States Policy. New
    York: National Association of Manufacturers, 1966.

Heppell, M. and Singleton, F. Yugoslavia. New York: Praeger, 1961.

Higgins, Benjamin. Economic Development. New York: W. W.
    Norton and Company, 1959.

Hirschman, Albert O. National Power and the Structure of Foreign
    Trade. Berkeley: University of California Press, 1945.

Hoeffding, Oleg. Recent Efforts Toward Coordinated Economic Plan-
    ning in the Soviet Bloc. P-1768. Santa Monica, Calif.: The
    RAND Corporation, August 1959.

_____. Recent Structural Changes and Balance of Payments Adjust-
    ments in Soviet Foreign Trade. P-3601. Santa Monica, Calif.:
    The RAND Corporation, May 1967.

Hoffman, George W. and Fred W. Neal. Yugoslavia and the New
    Communism. New York: Twentieth Century Fund, 1962.

Hondius, Frits W. The Yugoslav Community of Nations. The Hague:
    Mouton, 1968.

Horvat, Branko. An Essay on Yugoslav Society. Translated by
    Henry F. Mins. New York: International Arts and Sciences
    Press, 1969.

Institute of Comparative Law. The Foreign Trade, Foreign Exchange
    and Customs Systems. Belgrade: Federation of Jurists'
    Association, 1968.

Jovanovic, Aleksandar. The Social and Political System in Yugoslavia. Belgrade: Medunarodna Politika, 1966.

Kardelj, Edvard. On the Principles of the Preliminary Draft of the New Constitution of Socialist Yugoslavia. Belgrade: Jugoslavia Information Service, 1962.

Kaser, Michael. Comecon. London: Oxford University Press, 1967.

_____ (ed.) Economic Development for Eastern Europe. New York: St. Martin's Press, 1968.

Khudokormov, G. N. Political Economy of Socialism. Translated by Don Danemanis (ed.). Moscow: Progress Publishers, 1967.

Kohler, Heinz. Economic Integration in the Soviet Bloc. New York: Praeger, 1965.

Krause, Lawrence B. European Economic Integration and the United States. Washington, D.C.: The Brookings Institution, 1968.

Kravis, Irving B., and Robert E. Lipsey. The Use of Regression Methods in International Price Comparisons. Preliminary Paper. New York: National Bureau of Economic Research, 1967.

Lakicevic, Ognjen (ed.). A Handbook of Yugoslavia. Belgrade: Beogradski graficki zavod, 1969.

Leibenstein, Harvey. Economic Backwardness and Economic Growth. New York: John Wiley and Sons, 1957.

Lerner, Abba P. The Economics of Control. New York: The Macmillan Company, 1944.

Loucks, William. Comparative Economic Systems. New York: Harper and Row, 1965.

Macesich, George. Yugoslavia: The Theory and Practice of Development Planning. Charlottesville: The University Press of Virginia, 1964.

Machlup, Fritz. The Economics of Sellers' Competition. Baltimore: The Johns Hopkins Press, 1952.

Mandel, Ernest. Marxist Economic Theory. Translated by Brian
    Pearce. London: The Merlin Press, 1968.

Meade, J. E. The Balance of Payments. London: Oxford University
    Press, 1951.

_____. Trade and Welfare. London: Oxford University Press,
    1955.

Mendershausen, Horst. The Terms of Soviet-Satellite Trade: 1955-
    1959. RM-2507. Santa Monica, Calif.: The RAND Corporation,
    March 1962.

_____. The Terms of Trade Between the Soviet Union and Smaller
    Communist Countries, 1955-1957. RM-2305. Santa Monica,
    Calif.: The RAND Corporation, January 1959.

Michaely, Michael. Concentration in International Trade. Amsterdam:
    North-Holland Publishing Company, 1962.

Mikesell, R. and J. Behrman. Financing Free World Trade with
    the Sino-Soviet Bloc. Princeton Studies in International Finance,
    No. 8. Princeton, N.J.: Princeton University, 1958.

Ministry of Foreign Affairs of the Federal People's Republic of Yugo-
    slavia. White Book on Aggressive Activities by the Governments
    of the USSR, Poland, Czechoslovakia, Hungary, Rumania,
    Bulgaria and Albania Towards Yugoslavia. Belgrade.: The
    Ministry, 1951.

Montias, John Michael. Economic Development in Communist Rum-
    ania. Cambridge, Mass.: The MIT Press, 1967.

Moravec, Joze (ed.). Twenty Years of Yugoslav Economy. Belgrade:
    Medjunsrodna Stampa, 1967.

Muller, Kurt. The Foreign Aid Programs of the Soviet Bloc and
    Communist China. Translated by R. H. Weber and Michael
    Roloff. New York: Walker and Company, 1967.

Nagy, Imre. On Communism: In Defense of the New Course. New
    York: Praeger, 1957.

Neuberger, Egon. Central Planning and Its Legacies. P-3492. Santa
    Monica, Calif.: The RAND Corporation, December, 1966.

_____. The European Soviet Bloc and the West as Markets for
Primary Products. RM-3745. Santa Monica, Calif.: The RAND
Corporation, September 1963.

_____. International Division of Labor in CEMA: Limited Regret
Strategy. RM-3945. Santa Monica, Calif.: The RAND Corporation, December 1963.

_____. Soviet Economic Integration: Some Suggested Explanations
for Slow Progress. RM-3627. Santa Monica, Calif.: The RAND
Corporation, July 1963.

_____. The U.S.S.R. and the West as Markets for Primary Pro-
ducts: Stability, Growth and Size. RM-3341. Santa Monica,
Calif.: The RAND Corporation, February 1963.

Nove, Alec and Desmond Donneley. Trade with Communist Countries.
New York: The Macmillan Company, 1961.

Organization for Economic Cooperation and Development. Yugoslavia.
OECD Economic Surveys. Geneva: OECD, November 1969.

Pejovich, Svetozar. The Market-Planned Economy of Yugoslavia.
Minneapolis: University of Minnesota Press, 1966.

Pisar, Samuel. Coexistence and Commerce. New York: McGraw-
Hill Book Company, 1970.

Prybyla, Jan S. Comparative Economic Systems. New York: Appleton-Century-Crofts, 1969.

Pryor, Frederic L. The Communist Foreign Trade System. Cambridge, Mass.: The MIT Press, 1963.

Rip, Leon. Some Problems of the Yugoslav Economy. Belgrade.:
Jugoslavija, 1962.

Royal Institute of International Affairs Political and Economic Planning.
Economic Reform in Yugoslavia. Greenwich: Research Publications, July 1968.

Sawyer, Carole A. Communist Trade with Developing Countries:
1955-1965. New York: Praeger, 1966.

Scitovsky, Tibor. Economic Theory and Western European Integration. Stanford, Calif.: Stanford University Press, 1958.

Secretariat of the Economic Commission for Europe. The European Economy in 1965. New York: United Nations, 1966.

_____. The European Economy in 1967. New York: United Nations, 1968.

Shaffer, Harry G. (ed.). The Communist World: Marxist and Non-Marxist Views. New York: Appleton-Century-Crofts, 1967.

Siegel, Sidney. Choice, Strategy and Utility. New York: McGraw-Hill, 1964.

Spulber, Nicolas. The State and Economic Development in Eastern Europe. New York: Random House, 1966.

Stajner, Richard. At What Point Is the Reform. Belgrade: Stipe Duzevic, 1964.

Stigler, George. The Theory of Price. New York: The Macmillan Company, 1966.

Stojanovic, Rodmila (ed.). Yugoslav Economists on Problems of a Socialist Economy. Translated by Marco Pavicic. New York: International Arts and Sciences Press, 1964.

Stuart, Alan. Basic Ideas of Scientific Sampling. London: Charles Griffin and Company, 1964.

Tamedly, Elisabeth L. Socialism and International Economic Order. Caldwell, Idaho: The Caxton Printers, 1969.

Tornquist, David. Look East Look West. New York: The Macmillan Company, 1966.

Turgeon, Lynn. The Contrasting Economics. Boston: Allyn and Bacon, 1969.

U.S. Department of Commerce. Report of the U.S. Department of Commerce Trade Mission to Yugoslavia. August 31-October 16, 1959. Washington, D.C.: The Department, January 12, 1960.

United Nations, Economic Bulletin for Europe. New York: United Nations, November 1967.

Vakmanovic, Svetozar. Economic Reform in Yugoslavia. Translated by Jelena Hescog. Belgrade: Dnevnik, 1966.

Veljkovic, Ljubo (ed.). Economic Development in Yugoslavia. Belgrade: Medunarodna Stamps Interpress, 1968.

Viner, Jacob. Trade Relations Between Free-Market and Controlled Economies. Geneva: League of Nations, 1943.

Wiles, P. J. D. Communist International Economics. New York: Praeger, 1969.

Winsemius, A. and John Pincus (eds.). Methods of Industrial Development. Paris: Organisation for Economic Co-operation and Development, 1962.

Zaleski, Eugene. Planning Reforms in the Soviet Union, 1962-1966. Translated by Marie-Christine MacAndrew and G. Warren Nutter. Chapel Hill: The University of North Carolina Press, 1967.

Zaninovich, M. George. The Development of Socialist Yugoslavia. Baltimore: The Johns Hopkins Press, 1968.

Zsoldos, Laszlo. Economic Integration of Hungary into the Soviet Bloc. Columbus: The Ohio State University Press, 1963.

ARTICLES

Aleksic, Milan. "Foreign Trade Enterprises," Yugoslav Survey, VIII (November 1967), 91-96.

Allen, Robert Loring. "Economic Motives in Soviet Foreign Trade Policy," The Southern Economic Journal, XXV (October 1958), 189-201.

Ames, Edward. "International Trade Without Markets—The Soviet Case," American Economic Review, XLIV (December 1954), 791-807.

Anakioski, Dusan. "Foreign Trade in the Years of the Reform," Yugoslav Survey, X, 3 (August 1969), 71-84.

Bajt, Aleksander. "Yugoslav Economic Reforms, Monetary and Production Mechanism," Economics of Planning, VII, 3 (1967), 200-18.

Balassa, Bela. "Planning in an Open Economy," Kyklos, XIX, 3 (1966), 385-410.

Balazsy, Sandor. "Some Timely Questions Relating to the Economic Efficiency of Foreign Trade," Eastern European Economics, Summer 1963, pp. 28-35.

Bicanic, Rudolf. "Economics of Socialism in a Developed Country," Foreign Affairs, XLIV, 4 (1966), 633-50.

Borisenko A. and V. Shastitho. "Problems of the Economic Efficiency of Foreign Trade in the Socialist Countries," Problems of Economics, March 1963.

Brown, Alan. "Towards a Theory of Centrally Planned Foreign Trade." In Alan Brown and Egon Neuberger, eds., International Trade and Central Planning. Los Angeles: The University of California Press, 1968.

_____. and Egon Neuberger. "Foreign Trade of Centrally Planned Economics: An Introduction." In Alan Brown and Egon Neuberger, eds., International Trade and Central Planning. Los Angeles: The University of California Press, 1968.

Crawford, J. T. "Yugoslavia's New Economic Strategy: A Progress Report," Economic Developments in Countries of Eastern Europe. Joint Economic Committee, Congress of the United States, 1970.

Diachenko, V. "Main Trends in Improving Prices in Trade Among Comecon Members," Problems of Economics, June 1968, pp. 40-49.

Dupont, C. and F. A. G. Keesing. "The Yugoslav Economic System and Instruments of Yugoslav Economic Policy: A Note," International Monetary Fund Staff Papers, VIII (November 1960), 77-84.

Ellman, Michael. "Economic Reform in the Soviet Union," Political and Economic Planning. London: Royal Institute of International Affairs, April 1969.

Erlich, E. "International Comparisons by Indicators Expressed in Physical Units," Acta Oeconomica, 1967, pp. 107-22.

Fawcett, J. E. S. "State Trading and International Organization," Law and Contemporary Problems, XXIV (Spring 1959), 341-49.

Haberler, Gottfried. "Theoretical Reflections on the Trade of Socialist Economies." In Alan Brown and Egon Neuberger, eds., International Trade and Central Planning. Los Angeles: The University of California Press, 1968.

Hagen, Everett E. and Oli Hawrylyshyn. "Analysis of World Income and Growth, 1955-1965," Economic Development and Cultural Change, XVIII, 1, Part II (1969), 1-96.

Hazard, John N. "State Trading in History and Theory," Law and Contemporary Problems, XXIV (Spring 1959), 241-55.

Holzman, Franklyn D. "Discrimination in International Trade," American Economic Review, XXXIX, 6 (December 1949), 1233-44.

_____. "Foreign Trade Behavior of Centrally Planned Economies." In Morris Bernstein, ed., Comparative Economic Systems: Models and Cases. Homewood, Ill.: Richard D. Irwin, 1969.

_____. "More on Soviet Bloc Trade Discrimination," Soviet Studies, XVII (July 1965), 44-65.

_____. "Soviet Bloc Mutual Discrimination: Comment," Review of Economics and Statistics, XLIV (November 1962), 496-99.

_____. "Soviet Foreign Trade Pricing and the Question of Discrimination," Review of Economics and Statistics, XLIV (May 1962), 134-47.

Horvat, Branko. "Yugoslav Economic Policy in the Post War Period: Problems, Ideas, Institutional Developments," American Economic Review, LXI, 3 (June 1971), 69-169.

Humphrey, Don D. "The Economic Consequences of State Trading," Law and Contemporary Problems, XXIV (Spring 1957), 276-90.

Jancic, Lazar. "The New External Trade and Foreign Exchange System," Yugoslav Survey, VIII (November 1967), 91-96.

Johnson, Harry G. "Notes on Some Theoretical Problems Posed by the Foreign Trade of Centrally Planned Economies." In Alan

Brown and Egon Neuberger, eds., International Trade and Central Planning. Los Angeles: The University of California Press, 1968.

Kravis, Irving B. and Robert E. Lipsey. "International Price Comparisons by Regression Methods," International Economic Review, X (June 1969), 233-46.

Kutt, Aleksander. "Prices and the Balance Sheet in Soviet-Captive Countries Trade in 1961," Report Presented to the Assembly of Captive European Nations General Committee, Doc. 343 (April 1963), 83-100.

Lange, Oscar. "On the Economic Theory of Socialism," On the Economic Theory of Socialism. Edited by Benjamin E. Lippincott. Minneapolis: University of Minnesota Press, 1938.

Leontief, Wassily. "The Pure Theory of the Guaranteed Annual Wage Contract," Journal of Political Economy, LIV (February 1946), 76-79.

Lovitt, Craig E. "Soviet Economic Policy in Yugoslavia," Swiss Review of World Affairs, VIII (September 1958), 19-20.

_____. "Yugoslavia and the Soviet Union," Pakistan Horizon, XI (September 1958), 156-64.

"Market Factors in Yugoslavia," Overseas Business Reports. Washington, D.C.: U.S. Government Printing Office, May 1969.

Mazi, Milan. "Tourism, 1962-1967," Yugoslav Survey, IX, 1 (February 1968), 69-78.

Mendershausen, Horst. "A Final Comment," Review of Economics and Statistics, XLIV (November 1962), 499.

_____. "Mutual Price Discrimination in Soviet Bloc Trade," Review of Economics and Statistics, XLIV (November 1962), 493-96.

_____. "The Terms of Soviet-Satellite Trade: A Broader Analysis," Review of Economics and Statistics, XLII (May 1960), 152-63.

_____. "Terms of Trade Between the Soviet Union and Smaller
  Communist Countries, 1955-1957," Review of Economics and
  Statistics, XLI (May 1959), 106-18.

Michal, Jan M. "Czechoslovakia's Foreign Trade," Slavic Review,
  XXVII (June 1968), 212-29.

Montias, John Michael. "Economic Reform and Retreat in Jugoslavia,"
  Foreign Affairs, XXXVII, 2 (1957), 291-305.

Neuberger, Egon. "Central Planning and Its Legacies: Implications
  for Foreign Trade." In Alan Brown and Egon Neuberger, eds.,
  International Trade and Central Planning. Los Angeles: University of California Press, 1968.

"The New Yugoslav Foreign Exchange System," Ekonomska Politika
  (Economic policy). Translated by Joint Publication Research
  Service (JPRS). JPRS, no. 37, September 19, 1966, p. 692.

Nutter, G. Warren. "Trends in Eastern Europe," Economic Age, I
  (November-December 1968), 8-12.

Nyerges, Janos. "Some Thoughts on East-West Trade," Co-existence,
  IV (July 1967), 129-32.

Ouin, Marc. "State Trading in Western Europe," Law and Contemporary Problems, XXIV (Summer 1959), 398-419.

Pejovich, Svetozar. "Liberman's Reforms and Property Rights in
  the Soviet Union," The Journal of Law and Economics, XII
  (April 1969), 155-62.

Pertot, V. "Yugoslavia's Economic Relations with Eastern European
  Countries," Co-existence, IV (January 1967), 7-13.

Pryor, Frederic L. "Foreign Trade Theory in the Communist Bloc,"
  Soviet Studies, XIV (July 1962), 41-61.

Samardzija, M. and Radoslav Ratkovic. "Yugoslavia: A Yugoslav
  Marxist View." In G. G. Shaffer, ed., The Communist World:
  Marxist and Non-Marxist Views. New York: Meredith Pub-
  lishing Company, 1967, 260-93.

Savicevic, Milorad. "Protective Tariffs and Other Measures of
  Protection of the National Economy," Yugoslav Survey, XI
  (February 1970), 55-62.

Spulber, Nicolas. "The Soviet-Bloc Foreign Trade System," Law
    and Contemporary Problems, XXIV (Summer 1959), 420-34.

_____. and Franz Gehrels. "The Operation of Trade Within the
    Soviet Bloc," Review of Economics and Statistics, XL (May
    1958), 140-49.

Sretenovic, Mladen. "The Present System of Foreign Trade Regulation
    in Yugoslavia." Translated by Joint Publication Research Service
    (JPRS) from Nova Trgovina, September 1967, 418-21. JPRS,
    no. 43, p. 784.

Stolte, Stefan C. "Comecon on the Threshold of the Seventies,"
    Bulletin, Institute for the Study of the USSR, vol. XVIII (July
    1970).

"The System and Organization of Foreign Trade," Yugoslav Survey,
    IV (September 1963), 2029-41.

Viner, Jacob. "International Relations Between State Controlled
    National Economies," American Economic Review, XXXIV
    (March 1944), 315-29.

Wilczynski, J. "Dumping and Central Planning," The Journal of
    Political Economy, LXXIV (June 1966), 250-64.

Wilson, T. and G. R. Denton. "Plans and Markets in Yugoslavia,"
    in Royal Institute of International Affairs Political and Economic
    Planning, Economic Reform in Yugoslavia. London: Research
    Publications, July 1968.

Wszelaki, Ian. "Economic Developments in East-Central Europe,
    1954-1959," Orbis, IV (Winter 1961), 422-23.

Wyczalkowski, Marcin R. "Communist Economics and Currency
    Convertibility," International Monetary Fund Staff Papers,
    XIII (July 1966), 155-97.

                    UNPUBLISHED MATERIAL

Brown, Alan A. "The Economics of Centrally Planned Foreign Trade:
    The Hungarian Experience." Unpublished Ph.D. dissertation,
    Harvard University, 1966.

Marer, Paul. "Foreign Trade Prices in the Soviet Bloc: A Theoreti-
    cal and Empirical Study." Unpublished Ph.D. dissertation,
    University of Pennsylvania, 1968. University Microfilms.

Markovich, S. C. "The Influence of American Foreign Aid on Yugo-
    slav Policies, 1948-1966." Unpublished Ph.D. dissertation,
    University of Virginia, 1968.

Milenkovitch, Deborah Duff. "Planning and the Market in Yugoslavia."
    Unpublished Ph.D. dissertation, Columbia University, 1966.
    University Microfilms.

Pryor, Frederic L. "The Foreign Trade System of the European
    Communist Nations." Unpublished Ph.D. dissertation, Yale
    University, 1961.

Soskic, Branislav. "Current Problems in Economic Planning in
    Yugoslavia." Current Problems of Economic Planning in
    Eastern Europe. Thomas Jefferson Center, University of
    Virginia and CESES, Milan, Italy. Sorrento Seminar, July
    1968. (Mimeographed.)

Thomas Jefferson Center, University of Virginia and CESES, Milan,
    Italy. "Current Problems of Economic Planning in Eastern
    Europe." Sorrento Seminar, July 1968. (Mimeographed.)

_____. "Economic Reform in Foreign Trade in Eastern Europe."
    Grado Seminar, Italy, August 1970. (Mimeographed.)

_____. "Implementation of Economic Reforms in Eastern Europe."
    Venice Seminar, August 1969. (Mimeographed.)

STATISTICAL SOURCES

International Financial Statistics. International Monetary Fund
    (selected years).

Statisticki Godisnjak Jugoslavije. Belgrade: Federal Institute for
    Statistics (selected years).

Statistika Spoljne Trgovine SFR Jugoslavije. Belgrade: Federal
    Institute for Statistics (selected years).

Supplement to the World Trade Annual, vol. 1. New York: Walker
    and Company, 1967.

Yugoslav Foreign Trade Almanac, 1968. Belgrade: Yugoslavia-
    public, 1968.

ABOUT THE AUTHOR

RYAN C. AMACHER is Assistant Professor of Economics at the University of Oklahoma. He has been a consultant with General Electric, TEMPO, Center for Advanced Studies, and an International Economist with the Office of Trade Policy, U. S. Treasury.

Dr. Amacher received an A. B. from Ripon College and a Ph. D. from the University of Virginia.